With the Cavalry
to Afghanistan

With the Cavalry to Afghanistan

The Experiences of a Trooper
of H. M. 4th Light Dragoons
During the First Afghan War

William Taylor

LEONAUR

With the Cavalry to Afghanistan
by William Taylor
Troop Serjeant-Major of the
Fourth Light Dragoons

First published under the title
Scenes and Adventures in Afghanistan
1842

Leonaur is an imprint
of Oakpast Ltd

Copyright in this form © 2008 Oakpast Ltd

ISBN: 978-1-84677-568-0 (hardcover)
ISBN: 978-1-84677-567-3 (softcover)

http://www.leonaur.com

Publisher's Notes

In the interests of authenticity, the spellings, grammar and place names
used have been retained from the original editions.

The opinions of the authors represent a view of events in which he
was a participant related from his own perspective,
as such the text is relevant as an historical document.

The views expressed in this book are not necessarily
those of the publisher.

Contents

Preface   7

H. M. Light Dragoons   9

The Ameers of Scinde   19

Ambushes by Belochees   28

Perils of the March   37

Thief in the Night   44

Towards Ghuznee   51

The Fall of the Citadel   58

Incidents of the Battles   68

Dost Mohammed Flees   75

At Kabul   81

Reprisals   87

Journey to the Coast   94

Appendix   105

An Overview of the Afghan Campaign   113

Preface

The following narrative is put forth with all the diffidence and apprehension that a mind unaccustomed to literary pursuits, and limited in its opportunities of improvement, naturally feels on presenting itself for the first time to the notice of the public. The doubts I entertain, regarding the prudence of the step I have taken, are in no small degree increased by the circumstances under which the work has been executed, the details having been entirely furnished from memory, and without the aid of any sort of data or memoranda. I should never have dreamt of undertaking such a task, had not the partiality of good natured, though perhaps misjudging friends, overcame the scruples which a consciousness of my own deficiencies excited, and induced me to commit to paper the scenes with which they professed themselves to have been amused.

Having candidly admitted the demerits of the work, I may now be allowed to say a few words in its favour. Should it be taken up in the expectation of supplying materials for the defence of an erroneous policy, or the gratification of party spleen, it will fall short of the hopes of the reader, for I have endeavoured to steer clear of   everything like political allusion in the fear of adding to difficulties, which already appeared sufficiently formidable, and of wrecking my little bark on a stormy and troubled sea. Mine is the simple, straightforward narrative of a soldier, more accustomed to wield the sword than the pen, and caring little for the conflicting interests or animosities of party. With such a small amount of profession, it is not unreasonable to hope that the public will extend towards it some portion of

that generous indulgence with which it is ever wont to regard
the literary efforts of the humbler classes.

London, December 10th, 1842.

CHAPTER 1

H. M. Light Dragoons

Towards the latter end of August 1838, rumours reached Bombay and the various military-stations in the Deccan, that the troops were about to be called into active service, and that the scene of operations was to be at a distance from our Indian territories. The extensive preparations soon after set on foot, and the unusual activity observable in the various arsenals of the Presidency, left no doubt as to the truth of these reports, and the only subject of speculation that remained was, the precise destination of the forces. Public curiosity was at length set at rest, by the arrival of a proclamation from the Governor General, directing the assemblage of an army for service across the Indus, and explaining at length the intentions of Government.

It will not be necessary for the purposes of this narrative that I should canvass the merits of this remarkable document, or enter upon a discussion of the policy on which it was founded. Sufficient is it for me to say that the objects which it professed were the protection of our commerce, and the safety of our Indian frontiers, both of which were menaced by the intrigues and aggressions of Persia. Having detailed the steps taken by Dost Mahommed in furtherance of the views of that power, and expressed its conviction, that as long as Kabul remained under his government there was no hope that the interests of our Indian empire would be preserved inviolate, the proclamation proceeded to state, that pressing necessity, as well as every consideration of policy and justice, justified us in replacing on the throne of Afghanistan, Shah Soojah-Ool-Moolk, a monarch who, when in power, had cordially acceded to the measures of joint resistance to external aggression which were at that time judged necessary by the British government; and who on his empire being usurped by its present rulers had found an honourable asylum in the British dominions.

Such in a few words were the objects set forth in Lord Auckland's proclamation and never has unfortunate state paper been assailed with such hostility and bitterness. Whether the censures with which it has been visited are deserved or not I will leave to others to decide, contenting myself with the observation that failure and success are but too apt to sway men's judgements and to give a character to the circumstances that have led to them.

The Bombay troops ordered to form part of the army of the Indus consisted of Her Majesty's 2nd, or Queen's Royals, the 17th Regiment of Foot, 307 of Her Majesty's 4th Light Dragoons, the 1st Regiment of Bombay Light Cavalry, two troops of the Honourable Company's Horse Artillery, one company of foot artillery, the 19th regiment of Native Infantry, the Poona Irregular Horse, with the sappers and miners, the whole constituting an effective force of about 6,000 men, under the command of Lieutenant-General Sir John Keane.

The 4th Light Dragoons were stationed at Kirkee, about seventy miles from Bombay, when orders arrived that the detachment should proceed to the Presidency, for the purpose of embarking for its destination. We left our cantonments early in November, and overtook the artillery, which had preceded us from Poona, at the Ghauts. We halted here two days, and were joined by Her Majesty's 17th Regiment of Foot, shortly after our arrival. Short as was our stay, it was signalised by one of those practical jokes which so often terminate in fatal results, but which, unfortunately, seem to have no effect in rendering people cautious. Some artillerymen having been out shooting game, one of them brought home a loaded gun and carelessly left it in his tent. Several of his comrades came in, in the afternoon, and in the course of a carousal one of them took the loaded piece, and presenting it at the nearest soldier, jestingly threatened to shoot him. He had scarcely uttered the word when the gun went off and stretched his unfortunate comrade dead at his feet. Nothing could equal the distress and remorse of the homicide at the thoughtless act by which he had deprived a fellow creature of life, and it had a marked effect on his future character and conduct.

The passage through the Ghauts is romantic and picturesque in the extreme, the road lying over stupendous mountains and through deep ravines for the length of about seven or eight miles. Some beautiful country houses have been lately erected here by a wealthy Parsee of Bombay, on sites which command the finest and most extensive views in the neighbourhood. These delightful summer retreats are surrounded by every luxurious accessory that wealth and taste can supply, and the Governor is occasionally glad to fly to them for a short respite from the cares of office.

We arrived at Bombay on the 10th of November, and found it a scene of busy excitement. The streets were filled with troops and artillery proceeding to the place of embarkation, and the inhabitants flocked in thousands to the Bunder Head, to witness their departure. The harbour was literally alive with the numerous small craft employed in conveying the troops to the different transports, while the Blue Peter flying at the mast head of the latter announced that we had very little time for delay. We accordingly hurried down to the beach, and were immediately put on board the *Cambridge*. We found it so crowded that Major Daly, our commanding officer, was compelled to remonstrate with the authorities on the subject, and after some trouble, he succeeded in getting from seventy to eighty men removed to the other vessels. This did not sufficiently lessen the inconvenience to prevent sickness breaking out amongst us, and we lost one of the horse artillery before we were many days at sea.

The passage was short, but not unattended with danger. The *Cambridge* struck on a sand bank, off the Gulf of Cutch, and it was with considerable difficulty that she was relieved from her perilous position. We were kept on the bank about four hours, and it may easily be conceived that no small degree of alarm and uneasiness prevailed amongst the landsmen, who were unaccustomed to dangers of this description. The night was pitch dark, and the breakers sounded unpleasantly near us. Captain Douglass the commander of the vessel, appeared however all confidence, and after trying a variety of experiments to get her off, he hit upon one which luckily proved successful. The whole of the troops on board having been ordered upon deck, the captain directed them to jump three times simultaneously. This was done by our fellows with a hearty good will, and had the instant effect of loosening the vessel from the bank, and enabling her to float again into deep water.

We arrived off the mouth of the Indus in about fourteen days after our departure from Bombay. The troops were immediately disembarked in *pattemars,* small and clumsy coasting vessels peculiar to the country. We reached Bominacote the next evening without any other accident than the sinking of three boats, two containing artillery horses, and the other officers' supplies, to the value it was said of £10,000 which had been sent on speculation with the army by an eminent Parsee firm at Bombay.

Bominacote forms a sort of harbour of refuge for the vessels which carry on a trade along this line of coast. The village itself consists of a few filthy huts, and its inhabitants spend their lives in hunting and fishing. Both males and females are in a state of almost savage nature little covering being used by them beyond the loin *goity* or covering for the loins common to the natives of these parts. The proverbial vanity of the weaker sex was, however, displayed in the eagerness with which they bartered their most precious articles for a few handkerchiefs of Manchester make that we happened to have with us.

As soon as the horses belonging to the cavalry, and the military stores had been landed, it was decided that we should advance upon Scinde in two divisions; the infantry under the command of Brigadier Sir Thomas Wiltshire, and the cavalry under Brigadier Scott. Previous to our departure the troops were reviewed by Lieutenant-General Sir John Keane, who had followed us from Bombay in the *Victoria* steamer. Sir John expressed himself in terms of warm satisfaction at the high state of discipline and ardour of the men, who were eager to be led against the enemy. The usual precautions on entering hostile territories were now taken, the cavalry being ordered to sharpen their sabres, and the Infantry served with sixty rounds of ball cartridge.

Before we took our departure from Bominacote, a melancholy circumstance occurred, which threw a temporary gloom over us. As the men were sitting down to dinner the report of a pistol was heard in the officers' lines. Suspecting some accident I ran to the spot, accompanied by two of my comrades, and discovered Lieutenant Fyers, one of the officers of my own regiment, lying dead in his tent, with a freshly discharged pistol in his right hand. The unfortunate gentleman had placed the muzzle of it to his mouth, and the ball, taking a slanting direction, had passed out over the left ear. For several days previous he had been observed to labour under great depression of spirits, but no immediate cause could be assigned for the fatal act. His loss was generally lamented, for he was both a good officer and an estimable member of society.

Our route lay through a country barren in the extreme, scarcely a vestige of vegetation being anywhere to be met with. Of the natives we saw or heard nothing, for as we advanced they fell back, deserting the villages and betaking themselves to their mountain fastnesses. It being now near Christmas the men suffered some inconvenience from the sudden transitions of temperature, the days being sultry and the nights extremely cold. The consequence was that the dysentery broke out amongst us, and several fatal cases occurred.

At the close of the third days' march reports became current through the camp that we should soon see the enemy. It was said that a force of ten thousand horse and foot was about to take the field against us, and Captain Outram was despatched towards Hyderabad, to ascertain the truth of the story. He brought back information that the enemy were ensconced within the walls of that town, and appeared to have little disposition to leave them. We now began to find the difference between quarters and camp, for the General thought it necessary to send out frequent reconnoitring parties and pickets, in order to guard against surprise.

Early on the morning of the fifth day, we arrived at Tattah, a place of considerable antiquity, and, I believe, mentioned in Holy Writ. The Indus formerly washed the walls of this town, but owing to some natural or artificial ingredient the course of the river has been completely changed and it now rims at about four miles distance.

Emerging from one of the most barren and desolate tracts of country that it is possible to imagine, even the tombs of Tattah, or City of the Dead, as it is called in the language of the natives, proved an agreeable distraction to us. Tattah itself is a small, wretchedly built town, containing little more than a thousand inhabitants, who are for the most part of the Moslem religion. The few Hindoos who reside here constitute the wealthier part of the trading community, but influential as this fact would presuppose them, they are a persecuted and oppressed race, the privilege of erecting places of worship within the precincts of the town being not only denied them, but even the free exercise of their religious rites. Aggressions of the most wanton and tyrannical nature, and murders committed under circumstances of the most shocking barbarity, and having their origin solely in religious jealousy, are matters of no unfrequent occurrence here.

The Hindoos are consequently obliged to resort to the caves of the neighbouring mountains, to practise their religious ceremonies, but the relentless intolerance of their persecutors pursues them even there. During our short stay we saw the bodies of two of the proscribed race, who had been found murdered in one of their concealed temples.

The tombs of Tattah stand on a gentle eminence, at a short distance from the town: they are of circular construction, and are, as nearly as I could judge, from seventy to eighty feet in circumference, and from thirty to forty feet in height. They are capped with domes, but their external appearance presents nothing-graceful or ornamental to the eye. The interior is gained by a staircase, which ascends to an aperture forming the entrance, about midway in the building, and a rudely constructed ladder conducts the visitor downward to the basement, where the bodies lie. The interior of the dome is lined with blue tiles richly ornamented with arabesques and inscriptions from the Koran. There are about a dozen of these remarkable monuments and they are clustered together, without arrangement or regard for effect. Of the many sketches taken at the time I have not seen one which conveys a correct idea of their details. Although visited by nearly the whole of the troops, it is a fact highly creditable to their good taste and feeling that no mischief or desecration of any sort was committed. Sir John Keane, in a general order issued before our departure, took occasion expressly to allude to this circumstance, in terms alike honourable to himself and to us.

A curious, and I must say revolting, instance of the gross superstition of the Hindoos fell under my observation whilst at Tattah. At the northern extremity of the bazaar I was shown some of the most miserable specimens of humanity that can well be imagined. In a filthy mud hut, the very aspect of which threatened contagion, sat two living skeletons rocking themselves to and fro. They were without covering of any sort, except the old blanket on which they sat, and their deep sunk eyes and contracted features told a tale of long but patiently endured privation. I was informed that these poor wretches were undergoing a self-inflicted penance, for the non-performance of some religious rite. They had condemned themselves for a period of seven years to a daily allowance of rice and water, barely sufficient to prevent the extinction of the vital powers. We offered them food, but they sternly rejected it. This lamentable fanaticism on the part of a simple and inoffensive people is, after all, but another and more harmless phase of the fierce bigotry, which still continues to exist amongst European nations.

A *dâk,* or native postman, who had crossed the river from

15

Bhooj with letters for the camp, was waylaid by two Belochees as he was descending towards it, by the left bank, and the letter bag taken from him. His captors, having brought him to their retreat in the lulls, secured his hands behind his back, and lay down to sleep, one of them using the letter bag as a pillow. The *dâk* remained quiet, until their snoring satisfied him they were sound asleep, and then slipping his hands out of the ligatures, he stole over to the fellow who had the post-bag under him, and placing his knee on his breast, cut his throat from ear to ear with a knife, which he took from the mountaineer's person, and made off with the bag. In about ten minutes after, he heard the Belochee close upon his heels, and, redoubling his speed, a chase of nearly ten miles ensued, in the course of which, the poor fellow had two or three times nearly yielded from fatigue. The dreadful fate which awaited him, should he fall into his pursuer's hands, flashed however across his mind, and plucking up fresh strength and courage, he at length succeeded in reaching the camp, but in so weak and exhausted a state that nature was near sinking under the effort.

On the eve of our departure, a circumstance occurred which created a very angry feeling between the inhabitants and the troops, and occasioned much regret to the commander-in-chief, who was desirous that our advance should not be marked by anything which savoured of cruelty. In consequence of the great increase of drunkenness amongst the European troops, owing to the cheapness and abundance of liquor, strict orders were issued against its being allowed into camp. One of the inhabitants of Tattah, who was engaged in smuggling the prohibited article, was stopped about dusk by a serjeant, who happened to be going his rounds. The fellow took to his heels, and a sepoy, who was stationed as sentry in the staff lines, mistaking him for a thief, and seeing him pass at a speed which rendered capture out of the question, levelled his musket, and shot him dead on the spot. He was a fine muscular fellow, about two or three and twenty, and belonged to a respectable family in the town. His friends immediately repaired to the scene in a numerous body, and carried him off amidst the wailing and lamentation of the women. After this it was considered dangerous for any of us to venture into the town when nightfall had set in.

The army was now ordered to advance upon Jurruk, a town situated on the banks of the Indus, at about a day's march from Tattah. It is better built and cleaner than the latter place, and some of the streets are covered over with thatched roofs, forming a series of rude arcades, illuminated by oil lamps. Opthalmia is a common disease amongst the natives, and several of the troops were attacked by it. Some of us also suffered severely from the guinea worm, a malady, common in some parts of Hindostan, and which, although not considered dangerous, is attended with great pain. It generally attacks the feet, and has the effect of effectually crippling the patient for the time. I have had one drawn out of my right foot, which measured nearly half a yard in length, and I have known others to have had no less than from seven to eight of them at once. It being impossible for persons thus affected to march on foot or even to mount on horseback, they were usually carried along with the army in *kajarvees*, a sort of double-chair strung across the back of a camel, and swinging with a see-saw movement that occasioned no small additional suffering to the unfortunate occupant.

The spot selected for the encampment was extremely lovely, being encircled by hills, and having the River Indus running on its right. As the different regiments wound their way round the heights, and descended into the plain where the tents were to be pitched, the scene would have made a beautiful subject for a sketch. How often during a progress through this wild and romantic country have I regretted the want of a sufficient acquaintance with the art of design, to enable me to convey to paper some of its more striking and characteristic features.

In consequence of the numerous thefts committed by the Belochees, who daily carried off numbers of our camels, it became necessary to provide them with guards whilst at pasturage. This, however, did not prevent the plunderers from continuing their descents, and they became so hardy that they sometimes even ventured to attack or carry off the guards themselves. One day, whilst a party of the Poona Auxiliary Horse were in charge of some camels about two miles from camp, the Belochee came suddenly upon them. There were only six of our men, whilst the enemy numbered twelve or fifteen. Nothing daunted, however, a gallant fellow dashed out from amongst our men, and cut down three or four of the marauders. Being quickly seconded by the others, the Belochees took to flight, and the black hero dismounted, and cutting off the head of one of his dead antagonists, strung it by the hair to his crupper, and triumphantly rode into camp with it, amidst the acclamations of his comrades. A more substantial reward was conferred upon him for this daring exploit a few days afterwards by his promotion to the rank of *havildar* or serjeant. This may be said to have been the first occasion on which any of our troops came into actual collision with the enemy, but the example which was made had little or no effect in restraining the thefts of the Belochees who appeared to have an incorrigible taste for this sort of adventure.

CHAPTER 2

The Ameers of Scinde

A melancholy incident occurred at Jurruk, but whether it was occasioned by accident or treachery we never could satisfactorily trace. Some officers belonging to the Queen's Royals applied for leave to go hunting in the preserves of the *Ameers* of Scinde, and having obtained it, Lieutenant Sparkes, Lieutenant Nixon and Dr. Hibbert, who constituted the party, left the camp on foot at an early hour of the morning. Their leave of absence expired at six o'clock the same evening, but none of them had made their appearance at that hour. About half past eight a dog belonging to Dr. Hibbert was observed returning into camp without his master, which gave rise to gloomy apprehensions amongst his brother officers, and the non return of any of the party by next morning, confirmed their worst fears.

It was immediately determined to send out a troop of native cavalry to scour the country in search of them, and the preserves were of course the first spot to which they directed their horses. Part of the force dismounted at the *Shirkagh* or Royal Preserves, and proceeded on foot for a considerable distance. Observing smoke ascending in dense volumes to the right they made their way towards it, and on gaining the spot a shocking sight presented itself. A large area had been cleared by the flames, and not a blade of grass or brushwood had been left. The body of Lieutenant Sparkes lay, dreadfully scorched and mutilated, upon the ground, while that of Dr. Hibbert was found in a tree, into which he had evidently climbed to escape the devouring element. A little further on lay Lieutenant Nixon whose features were so withered and defaced, that it was almost impossible to recognize him, and from the contracted and distorted position in winch his limbs were found it was evident that he had suffered a more agonizing death than the others.

The remains of the three unfortunate officers were borne back to the camp and interred with military honours. They were all talented and spirited young men and their untimely fate was a source of universal regret and discussion. By some it was contended that the natives had observed them entering the preserves, and inspired by hate had fired the woods in different places, so as effectually to surround them and cut off all chance of escape. To such a degree did this supposition obtain credence, that the soldiers of the Queen's Royals loudly demanded to be allowed to take revenge on the inhabitants of the district. This of course could not be permitted, and the clamour that had been raised about the matter soon died away.

Shortly after our arrival an order came down from the *Ameers* of Scinde, that the inhabitants of Jurruk should vacate the town and retreat to Hyderabad. It was obeyed with great reluctance, the love of home being stronger with these poor people than their fear of the British. Their removal was one of the most distressing and painful scenes I have ever witnessed, both men and women giving way to wild bursts of passionate grief, and casting back long and lingering regards at the habitations they had abandoned. They left in bodies of between two and three hundred, carrying with them all their portable effects, and at night the town was completely deserted, We neither interfered with, nor molested them during their preparations for departure, but immediately on their quitting, a strong picket was posted in some of the empty houses.

Provisions became extremely scarce in the camp, and owing to the remissness of the commissariat in forwarding the stores from Tattah, our grog was reduced from two drams daily, to one dram on halting days. This was attended with the worst possible effects, for it encouraged the troops to search after the liquor of the country; which proved not only injurious to the constitution of the soldier, but to the discipline of the service. Desertion became of frequent occurrence, and from one hundred to one hundred and fifty camel drivers from India, together with some *Ghorra Wallars*, or native horse-keepers, succeeded in making their way across the river to Cutch Bhooj. A few were caught, and from six to twelve dozen lashes each were inflicted on the delinquents. Captain Outram was again sent forward to Hyderabad on a mission to the *Ameers* of Scinde, but they received him in the haughtiest manner and refused to come to any sort of terms.

The captain found them fortifying the hills round the city, under the superintendence of a European officer, and he observed a battery of twenty pieces of cannon, posted on the banks of the river. Twenty thousand Belochees armed with *talwar*, shield, and matchlock, and two thirds of whom were dismounted, occupied a position on the right bank, so as to protect the battery. Half of this force subsequently moved across the river and took up a strong position on the western bank, where we lay. The city was reported to be full of armed men, and the idea of attacking it previous to our junction with the Bengal army was regarded as worse than folly, the river being eighteen hundred feet wide and our pontoons of insufficient length to traverse it. The enemy, triumphing in our seeming inaction, sent vaunting and threatening messages to us.

The commander-in-chief took no notice of their bravadoes, but silently made all the necessary preparations for attacking the city as soon as he was joined by the Bengal army. Strong cavalry pickets were thrown out on the hills to the right, which commanded an extensive view of the surrounding country, and the sound of drums and other military instruments was strictly prohibited in camp.

On the 25th, Sir Henry Pottinger came into camp from Hyderabad, the *ameers* not only refusing to pay the arrears of tribute that were due, but treating the Envoy with every sort of indignity. The Bengal army having come through the Punjaub, and crossed the Indus at Roree was now ready to act in conjunction with us on the right bank of the river, and the commander-in-chief resolved to lose no further time in investing the city. He accordingly commenced operations by planting a battery on some heights which commanded its walls, but which were at too great a distance for the guns to do much damage. To the great disappointment of both officers and men, who already revelled in the anticipation of prize money, the *ameers* became alarmed at these demonstrations and came to terms. An envoy, whose appearance created no small amusement in the camp, was despatched from Hyderabad to adjust the necessary preliminaries. He was a short, thick set old fellow, with a merry twinkling eye, and as little as possible of what is called official dignity about him. He brought with him from twenty to thirty *lacs* of *rupees*, but the reception which he met with from Sir John Keane was not calculated to elevate the worthy functionary in his own estimation.

Positive orders having been issued that neither officers nor men should be allowed to enter Hyderabad on any pretence whatsoever, I am unable to give my readers a description of the town. It appeared to be of considerable extent, but of such little strength, that had the *ameers* driven matters to extremities, I have no doubt we should have carried the place in an hour.

We were exceedingly amused at the surprise and consternation displayed by the inhabitants of Hyderabad at the arrival of one of the iron steamers in the Indus, with supplies for the troops from Bombay. Nearly the whole of the population flocked down to the banks of the river to behold this surprising phenomenon; they threw their arms in the air, and flung themselves prostrate on the earth in perfect ecstasies of wonder at every movement of the mysterious power which propelled the vessel. The scene was nearly as ridiculous as that which greeted Columbus when the first notions of European power and civilisation burst upon the astonished minds of the simple aborigines of America.

After remaining a few days at Hyderabad the army resumed its march, and arrived next evening at Baida. An accident occurred here, by which a trooper of the 4th Light Dragoons lost his life. The banks of the river were extremely steep, and as we were watering our horses the pressure from behind forced a man named Helm into the river. He was instantly carried away by the current, and was soon lost to view, although we strained every effort to save him. His body floated down to Hyderabad, and was recovered by the natives, who restored it to his commanding officer, together with a belt full of *rupees*, which was found round his waist.

Continuing our route we arrived at the Lukkee Pass, where we found some thermal springs, from which the sick derived considerable benefit. A noble lake at the further extremity of the defile afforded our officers several days shooting and fishing, while the beautiful scenery, by which it was surrounded on every side, furnished such of them as were artists with fine subjects for the exercise of their pencil. Precipitous heights, assuming every variety of fantastic form, stretched downward to the water's edge, some in graceful sweeps, and others in bold and threatening attitudes, whilst their bases were hid in rich woods or washed by the waters of the lake.

Leaving this romantic spot with regret, we proceeded to Kotiah, where we lost two soldiers belonging to her Majesty's 17th Regiment of Foot. They went out in search of some camels which were at pasturage and were never afterwards seen or heard of. A party which was sent in search of them found the marks of footsteps and some traces of blood on the spot where the camels had been grazing, and from the torn up appearance which the ground presented there was little doubt that they had made a desperate struggle for their lives.

Not satisfied with carrying off our camels, the Belochees frequently ventured within the lines after nightfall, and made off with anything they could lay their hands upon. Sir Keith Jackson, the captain of my own troop, detected a fellow with a bridle in his hand, which he was watching an opportunity to slip off with unperceived, and taking his hand whip he inflicted a most unmerciful castigation upon him. The rascal whined and moaned like a corrected child during the progress of the punishment, but as soon as he was let loose he stuck his tongue in his cheek, and went laughing out of camp.

Our next destination was Sehwan, a thickly populated village, about seventy English miles from Hyderabad. Here we were joined by the ever to be lamented Sir Henry Fane, who was to have assumed the command of the combined forces at their junction at Kandahar, but who declined it in disgust at the wretchedly organised state of the commissariat, and the neglect which had been shown in providing for the contingencies of the route. Sir Henry foresaw, and subsequent events justified his views, that although supplies might be regularly forwarded from time to time, it was extremely doubtful, nay almost next to impossible, that they could reach an army always on the advance, through distant and mountainous regions, and having enemies hanging on its rear who were but too deeply interested in preventing their safe arrival.

Before Sir Henry left us he inspected the troops, and appeared satisfied with the condition of the men, who had not as yet encountered hardships sufficient to affect their appearance. There have been few men in command whose personal qualities have more endeared him to those who served under him than Sir Henry Fane. He was between sixty and seventy years of age, at the time I speak of, and his venerable countenance, beaming with the kindliest and most benevolent feelings, and manners that had a parental touch about them, combined to render him one of the most respected and popular officers in the army. We viewed his departure from amongst us with the deepest regret, for though we felt the fullest confidence in our then leader, this gallant veteran had so won upon our affections that a comparison with him must have proved invidious to anyone.

The ingenuity of the Asiatic jugglers is well known, and I believe our European exhibitors derive their proficiency, in a great measure, from them, our soldiery carrying back with them the rudiments of this respectable branch of knowledge, and turning their swords, if not into ploughshares, at least into as peaceable and innocent a mode of gaining a livelihood. An exhibition which took place during our short stay at Sehwan made many of the "greenhorns" amongst us gape, and impressed them with a very high notion of the favour in which the professors of the art are held by his Satanic Majesty. Returning one day from the bazaar, I observed a crowd of soldiers and natives assembled near the lines of the artillery.

Elbowing my way through them I found a conjurer at his tricks, and from the expensive and elaborate nature of the paraphernalia by which he was surrounded, at once perceived that his pretensions were of the highest order. He was attired in loose flowing robes, covered with mystic characters; and a long white beard descended to his waist, contrasting oddly with his jet black locks and piercing hazel eyes. Surrounded by the various emblems and accessories of his art, he looked a very imposing figure, and every movement which he made was regarded with as much interest as if destiny really rested on his fiat. His only assistants were a man who beat a *tom-tom,* or drum, to collect an audience, and a beautifully formed girl about five or six years of age, whose supple and graceful movements excited general admiration.

Having made a clear space of about thirty feet in diameter, the conjurer took an oblong basket, about two feet in length, and one in breadth, the interior of which he exhibited to the spectators, in order to convince them that nothing was concealed in it. After performing a variety of common-place tricks, such as balancing a sword upon a pipe and then swallowing the blade, he suddenly turned towards the child and addressed her in an angry tone of voice. She made some reply which appeared to make him still more choleric, for his features became swollen with rage, and his eyes shot glances of fire. The discussion continuing in the same violent strain he appeared no longer able to control his fury, and suddenly seizing the child by the waist, he opened the basket and crammed her into it.

The half stifled cries of the girl were distinctly heard, but they only appeared to enrage him the more. Snatching a sword, which lay near him, he plunged it to the hilt in the basket, twice or thrice, and every time he drew it out it was reeking with gore. The half smothered groans and sobs of the dying child at length convinced several of the spectators that a murder had been committed, and two or three soldiers rushed into the circle for the purpose of seizing the criminal. Triumphantly smiling at the success of the cheat, he held them at bay with the sword for a few minutes, when, to our great surprise, the child bounded into the circle, unscathed, from amidst the crowd, though we had kept our eyes attentively fixed on the basket all the time. Suspecting that two children had been employed, I examined the basket, but found no trace of an occupant, and saw nothing in its construction which could have aided the deception. This clever trick was loudly applauded, and brought its author a plentiful harvest of *pice* and *cowries*, while many there were who went away with the firm conviction that it could only have been effected through the agency of the devil himself.

We had left a number of sick behind us at Tattah, with instructions that they should be conveyed in *pattemars* up the river Indus, and rejoin us at Sehwan. A boat containing a corporal and five men was stranded on the banks of the river, and was with some difficulty got off. The soldiers were so prostrated with fever that they could scarcely move, and in this state they arrived at Sehwan. To their great distress they found that the army had proceeded on its route, and one of their companions expired immediately after their arrival. The heat of the sun was intolerable, and the corpse began to putrefy. In vain they implored the native boatmen to inter it or cast it in the river, but they preferred running the risk of infection to touching the dead body of an infidel.

The corporal, who was well acquainted with the language of the country, entreated some of the natives who crowded to the banks to remove the body, but they remained deaf to his prayers. Resorting to a stratagem which he thought would have the effect of removing their religious scruples, he asserted that the deceased had died in the Mohammedan faith, and commanded them on pain of the displeasure of the Prophet, to give him decent interment. At first they looked incredulous, but the corporal swore loud and fast, and they were at length convinced. They removed the body, and placing it on a sort of bier, somewhat similar to a sailor's hammock, carried it on shore. Having swathed it in cotton cloths, and laid it with the feet towards the setting sun, they decked the head and breast with flowers, and bore it in procession to the place of interment, which was situated in a romantic spot on the banks of the Indus. The companions of the deceased proceeded on their route, rejoicing in the success of the corporal's trick, and rejoined the main body without further accident.

Chapter 3

Ambushes by Belochees

Leaving Sehwan we crossed the Indus in pontoons, and entered a fertile tract of country. Our route lay through rich pasturage and waving fields of corn, occasionally diversified by rivers and lakes, the latter of which we found well stocked with fish and game. The natives did not exhibit any symptoms of fear at our approach, but continued peaceably tilling and cultivating their lands. Proceeding by rapid marches we at length reached Larkhana, the boundary which divides Upper and Lower Scinde. It is a place of considerable importance, and contains from seven to eight thousand inhabitants. Long cloths are manufactured here in considerable quantities, and a brisk trade is carried on, in various other articles with the mountain tribes. Sir John Keane now quitted us to proceed to Kandahar, where he was to assume the command of the Grand Army of the Indus. He was accompanied by two squadrons of native cavalry, one *rassalah* of Local Horse, a regiment of native infantry, and two pieces of artillery. The command of this division consequently devolved upon Major General Wiltshire.

The Belochees again favoured us with a visit and carried away about a dozen camels from the encampment. A troop of cavalry was ordered out in pursuit, and after a hot chase succeeded in coming up with the marauders. They immediately abandoned their prey and made off to the hills, but not before they had left three or four of their party in our hands. Resolved to make an example which would deter them from repeating the offence, General Wiltshire ordered the cat to be liberally administered to them in the bazaar.

The senior of the party was first tied up, and it was evident, from the trepidation he was in, that he expected no less than the punishment of death. He begged and implored for mercy, and finding that no attention was paid to his supplications, he took leave of one of the other culprits, who turned out to be his son, and resigned himself to die. Tied up, as he was, and unable to observe the expression of our countenances, which were con-vulsed with laughter, in anticipation of the scene that was about to follow, he every moment expected to hear the report of the musket, or feel the blow of the sabre that was to deal out his doom. The moment, however, the cat descended on his shoul-ders, the terrified expression of his face changed into that of the most extravagant joy. He smiled and nodded at his son, and bore his four dozen lashes with the joyful patience of a martyr, suf-fering in the vindication of some holy cause.

On being set loose the culprits were informed that if they were ever again detected in the commission of similar offences they would be shot, without mercy, and they were ordered to disseminate this useful piece of information amongst their com-rades of the hills.

Pursuing our route from Larkhana we encamped the same evening at Dooson, and were visited during the night by a ter-rific hurricane. Arising without any previous indication, the tempest came suddenly upon us in our sleep, sweeping the tents before it, and enveloping us in whirlwinds of white sand. The night being pitch dark we were soon in the greatest distress and confusion, and to add to our embarrassments the horses broke loose and ran wild amongst us. They killed two of the camp fol-lowers, and injured several others by treading them under foot, and the alarm which they created was as great as if the enemy had made a sudden irruption amongst us. To this succeeded a scene of rioting and squabbling, one having lost a shako, another a jacket, and another his shoes. Accusations and denials, oaths, vociferations, and complaints of injuries received, formed altogether a pleasant medley; and glad enough we were when the first streak of dawn threw some light on this scene of horrible confusion. After lasting about two hours, heavy drops of rain announced the approaching cessation of the tempest, but we only exchanged one discomfort for another, being soon drenched to the skin.

After two days further march we arrived at a wretched village, which separates Upper Scinde from Belochistan, and which is only entitled to notice as forming the boundary of a desert plain, about fifty miles in extent, and completely divested of vegetation, the white soil lying exposed to, and reflecting back with intensity, the scorching rays of the sun. There were only two wells at the village, and there was a fierce contest for precedence at them, it being known that there was neither spring nor stream of any kind in the desert which we were about to traverse. The infantry entered on this cheerless waste about three in the afternoon and the cavalry followed about five. The former were fully accoutred, and carried sixty rounds of ball cartridge each.

At two o'clock the following morning the cavalry overtook them and the general halt sounded. So great was the fatigue of the infantry that numbers threw themselves upon the ground in despair, declaring, it was impossible for human nature to sustain more, and they could proceed no further. It must be borne in mind that our rations had, for two months previous, consisted of only half a pound of flour and an equal quantity of red rice, with about four ounces of meat, and the latter was in some instances of no use to us, from the difficulty of procuring fuel to cook it.

The order of march having been again given, several refused to move from sheer exhaustion, and their situation became one of great embarrassment to their colonel, who was aware that if he left them behind, they would be instantly sabred by the enemy, who were always hovering on our rear. Recollecting it was St. Patrick's Day, and that most of the recusants were Irishmen, he ordered, as a last resource, that the band of the regiment should strike up their national anthem. The effect was electrical, the poor devils, whose limbs, a short time previous, had refused to perform their accustomed office, and whose countenances wore the aspect of the most abject despondency, seemed at once to have new life and energy infused into them. They felt that this was an appeal to their proverbial bravery and powers of endurance, and gratified vanity did that which threats and remonstrances had failed to effect. A faint smile lit up their features, and slowly rising from the ground they tottered on their way. Had they adhered to their first determination they would have fallen victims to the most savage cruelties, as the following circumstance will soon convince the reader:—

Three of the cooks belonging to our division, who followed with the camp kettles at a short distance in its wake, lost their way in the darkness of the night, and as chance would have it, stumbled upon a party of the enemy. They were immediately seized, and each man was bound by the wrist to the saddle of a Belochee horseman. The cries of the unfortunate men having reached the rear-guard, which consisted of the native auxiliary horse, they turned in pursuit, and soon came in sight of the enemy, whose figures were dimly visible in the obscurity which prevailed. As soon as they heard them galloping up the Belochees spurred their horses to their utmost speed, dragging their prisoners along with them at a terrific pace. Finding their pursuers gained upon them they stooped down, and with their broad knives ripped up two of their victims from the abdomen to the throat, and then cast them loose. The third, more fortunate, escaped with life, the Belochee to whose saddle he was attached having freed him by cutting off his left arm with a blow of his sabre: then wheeling round on our horse, who were now almost up with them, the enemy took deliberate aim at the advancing troopers, and having killed two, and severely wounded another, they plunged into the darkness and succeeded in baffling pursuit.

We reached the extremity of this barren waste by seven o'clock next morning, and encamped at the bottom of a steep hill where there was abundance of excellent water. The cupidity of the inhabitants of the neighbouring villages, having got the better of their apprehensions, several of them ventured into the camp with supplies of flour, which was eagerly purchased from them by the soldiery, at the rate of about half a crown the lb. The risk which they ran was great, for if the fact had been discovered, they would, in all probability, have been massacred by the mountain chief. The profits which they realised by the adventure, must however, have well repaid them for the hazard.

Descending the hills to our right, we one day observed a funeral procession; and curious to witness the ceremonies performed on those occasions I followed at a little distance. The corpse was swathed in cotton bandages like a mummy, the head only being left exposed, and it was borne on a bamboo bier, or stretcher, on the shoulders of four men. The relations and friends of the deceased gave vent to their grief in the bitterest lamentations, and there appeared a depth and sincerity in their woe which is but too often wanting at our European rites. The procession was headed by a *faquir* or priest, whose rolling eyes, and long dishevelled locks, gave him a wild and unearthly appearance. His costume was no less singular than his looks, for it consisted of a motley sort of garment, composed of patches of almost every coloured cloth, with a cap or rather a crown of peacock's feathers. Arrived at the place of interment, which was situated in the valley, the procession halted at a freshly dug grave, and the bier was laid beside it.

The crowd formed themselves into a circle round it, and the *faquir* holding up a small idol, commenced an oration in which he expatiated on the merits of the deceased. The crowd having prostrated themselves, the *faquir* took a reddish sort of powder, and made a large mark with it on the forehead of the dead man; then taking a basket of freshly pulled flowers and herbs he scattered them over the body and into the grave. The mourners rising from the ground, and walking in single files round the bier made a respectful salaam towards it, after which the corpse was lowered perpendicularly into the earth, and the grave filled up. At the conclusion, the *faquir* sat himself on a stone at a short distance from the grave, and remained there quietly smoking his hookah, and philosophising, as all good *faquirs* should do, on the uncertainty of mundane things.

Our next destination was Dadur, where we were to form a junction with a portion of the Bengal forces. The distance is only a day's march, and nothing of interest occurred on the route. On approaching the encampment of the Bengal troops, I could not help being struck with their superior appearance. It was evident that their commissariat was better organized than ours, for their camp equipage and other appointments were in all respects complete, and they were abundantly supplied with necessaries of every kind. This disparity was, in some degree, removed before we left Dadur, by the arrival of additional supplies from Bombay.

A few days having been passed in recruiting our strength after these fatiguing marches, we at length received orders to advance on the celebrated Bholun Pass. Nothing could be more calculated to awaken us to the difficulties of our position, or to impress us with the uncertainty of the fate that awaited us, than the imposing grandeur of the scenery on which we now entered. Let the reader picture to himself a gloomy looking gorge winding through two ranges of stupendous hills, whose rugged masses of rock and hanging declivities impend over the narrow route as if about to choke it up, or recede a short distance to some fortress-like looking freak of nature from whose imaginary bastions and parapets it seemed easy to hurl down destruction and death on the passenger, and he may easily imagine that our feelings were not of the liveliest or most comfortable nature.

A handful of men could have effectually stopped our progress had there been but another Leonidas amongst the wild inhabitants of this magnificent defile, whose military skill and resolution would have enabled him to seize upon, and maintain its many points of defence. We could not conceal from ourselves difficulties so apparent, and a general and undefined feeling of uneasiness pervaded us all. We felt that if the enemy had any intention of resisting us they would not lose opportunities which nature herself appeared to indicate; and it was but too obvious that if they only knew how to avail themselves of the formidable barriers which she had placed against invasion, our situation would become critical in the extreme. Once involved in the intricacies of the pass, the superior knowledge of the country possessed by the natives, and their familiarity with mountain warfare would enable them to harass us at every step, and a well planned and daring attack might at once overwhelm us. Such were the reflections that suggested themselves to almost every man's mind, and many there were, I dare say who just then thought of home, and speculated whether it would ever be his lot to revisit its peaceful fireside, and recount the dangers of which he had been the hero.

The Bengal troops who preceded us through the pass left behind them sad proofs of the justice of some of these conclusions. We found from five and twenty to thirty camp followers lying dead upon their track, the throats of several having been cut, and the others bearing on their mutilated persons the unequivocal evidence of a desperate hand to hand struggle. As we advanced through the gorge we could observe the Belochees peering at us over the jutting points of the precipices, and the sharp report of their gingalls and matchlocks, which, luckily for us, were not very sure in their aim, usually followed the brief inspection by which we were favoured. Observing a camp follower leading a camel at some distance in the rear, three of the mountaineers suddenly darted from a fissure in the rock in which they had lain concealed, and having cut the poor fellow down, led the animal up the ascent by one of those diverging tracks like sheep walks, with which these hills abound. A serjeant belonging to the horse artillery, who happened to witness the circumstance, instantly galloped back, and gallantly dashing his horse up the mountain succeeded in sabering the nearest of the thieves, and brought back the camel amidst a shower of balls from the neighbouring heights.

Within a few miles of the Afghanistan boundary the gorge

is traversed by a stream which winds like a snake through the sinuosities of the pass, and crosses it no less than sixteen times. Although it presents for the most part, the appearance of an insignificant mountain rivulet, it is, in many places studded with deep and dangerous holes, into which the cavalry often plunged, and got a good sousing before they were aware of it. Shouts of laughter usually escaped the comrades of the luckless wight who became thus involved, and on one occasion a tragedy had nearly resulted from their ill-timed merriment. An Irish trooper, named Dwyer, a brave, but hot-blooded fellow, like most of his countrymen, was feeling his way cautiously through the stream, when both horse and rider stumbled, and became instantly lost to view. Some alarm was at first experienced for their safety, but it gave way to a roar of laughter when we beheld them again emerging from the water. After several successive attempts to disengage himself, the horse at length obtained a secure footing, and Dwyer, wheeling him suddenly round upon us with a countenance furious with rage, drew a pistol from his holster and fired at a group of seven or eight men, who stood close to the spot, but fortunately without effect. The madman was immediately placed under arrest, but was released after a few days' confinement.

On approaching Beebenaunce towards the close of the fourth day's march, we found another stream where the cavalry dismounted, for the purpose of filling their canteens with water, while the Infantry were distributed so as to protect them. We had been marching for several hours under a scorching sun, and over a stony and rugged road, which rendered constant watchfulness and exertion necessary to prevent the horses from falling on their knees. Tormented by an insatiable thirst, we were about to slake it, when it was discovered that the stream was polluted by the putrefying bodies of several of dead Afghans, and followers of the Bengal army; the spot having been the scene of a deadly contest which had occurred some days previous. The struggle between the loathing which this circumstance created and the pressing calls of nature was however of short duration. Not a man of us hesitated to drink from the contaminated liquid, but the horse which I rode, being imbued with keener senses than his master, positively refused to partake of it, though almost dropping with fatigue and thirst. I took him lower down the stream, where his fastidiousness being no longer offended he indulged in a long and copious draught.

CHAPTER 4

Perils of the March

We were about to quit the pass at the close of the eighth day's march, when the enemy made another and more successful attempt at plunder. Emboldened by the absence of the Infantry, which was at a considerable distance in the rear, they descended the heights in greater numbers than usual, and attacked the camp followers in charge of the officers' baggage. The latter took to flight, and the Belochees commenced pillaging the trunks and cases. Amongst the property carried off was a camel belonging to Brigadier Scott, which was laden with the whole of the general's kit. A party of the 4th Dragoons, under the command of Lieutenant Gillespie, at length galloped up and put the enemy to flight. There were only three men wounded and three horses killed on our side, whilst the Belochees left great numbers of dead on the ground.

During the heat of the firing a mistake occurred, which at first occasioned some alarm, but was soon converted into a burst of uncontrollable merriment. Our men had driven the last of the enemy up the hill, the latter peppering away at them from every rock or crevice where they could find shelter, when our attention was arrested by the appearance of a general officer on the heights to our left, who appeared to be making signs to us. It was at first supposed that one of our leaders had fallen into the hands of the enemy, and universal consternation prevailed. The general at length took off his shako, and advancing to the very edge of the precipice, waved it in the air as if to cheer us on to his rescue, when to our infinite amusement we discovered it was the fellow who had made off with the Brigadier's kit, and who, after examining the contents of it, had rigged himself out in full uniform. The rocks echoed with laughter, and the *pseudo* general appeared to enjoy the fun as much as any of us, for he capered about in a perfect ecstasy of delight, and gave expression to his contentment in the most delectable yells. A shower of balls was at length directed against him, and the Brigadier's swarthy representative came tumbling down the precipice to render himself and his briefly enjoyed honours into our hands.

Amongst the booty carried off upon this occasion were the wind instruments belonging to the 1st Bombay Cavalry, and a bullock, carrying two packages of ball ammunition, which contained 500 rounds each. Some amusement was created amongst us by speculations as to the probable use that would be made of the former, the humour displayed in the appropriation of General Scott's kit having given us a high idea of the waggish propensities of the enemy. Our fun was however turned into mortification when we beheld them cutting our ball ammunition into slugs to fit the bore of their gingalls, and sending it back to us from the heights in as wholesale quantities as they had taken it.

In the course of the skirmish a feat was performed by two of the native troops, which was watched with the most intense interest. A Bruhee (a fierce and warlike tribe, distinguished by their inveterate hostility towards the black troops in our service,) had taken shelter behind a rock, about midway up the mountain, and kept up a constant fire on some native cavalry beneath. Two of the sepoys belonging to the Bombay native infantry observing the circumstance, determined on effecting his capture, and laying down their muskets at the foot of the hill, they crept stealthily up. Whenever the fellow's flashing eyes were observed on a line with the rock, searching for an object for his aim, they crouched under cover until the discharge of his gingall satisfied them he was about to reload. They then rapidly advanced to his lurking place, and pouncing suddenly upon him conveyed him down the hill.

The prisoner had such a horror of falling into our hands that he several times implored his captors to put an end to him on the spot. They took no notice of his entreaties until they had reached the bottom of the hill, where they had laid their arms, when a *havildar* meeting them inquired if they had not heard of the orders, that no prisoners should be brought into camp. "I knew nothing about it," replied one of the soldiers; "but this I do know that he is a stout-hearted fellow, and deserves a better fate."

"I understand you," exclaimed the other sepoy, and taking his musket he placed the muzzle of it to the prisoner's head, and literally covered the serjeant with his brains.

The quantity of carrion which we everywhere left upon our route attracted numbers of the ravening beasts of prey with which these hills abound, and we could not rest at night from the dismal howling which surrounded us. Even the new made graves of our comrades did not escape the keen and hungering scent of the jackal, their remains being scarcely interred before we found them again torn up, their whitening bones alone attesting the nature of the visitation. Amongst the greatest of our annoyances, however, was the intolerable stench which proceeded from the putrefying bodies of the camels, that lay scattered everywhere upon our track, and which was enough to breed a mortality.

As we emerged from the pass into the open country, the heights became literally alive with Belochees, who gave expression to their rage and disappointment in the most absurd and violent gesticulations. We bivouacked late at night in the open plain, after a fatiguing and harassing march of twelve hours, during which we had been unable to procure a drop of water. The same privation awaited us in the place where we passed the night, and the sufferings of both men and cattle were dreadful. It was not until six o'clock next day that we fell in with a stream that traversed the road to Quetta, and were able to satisfy the thirst which consumed us. We were now in the valley of Shawle, which presented a most agreeable contrast to the barren hills through which we had just passed: here we found a succession of vast orchards, whose fruit trees bursting into blossom and gladdening the wearied eye with a variety of the most beautiful tints recalled to most of us the pleasant scenery of dear old England.

On our arrival at Quetta the troops underwent a medical inspection, and it was determined that the sick should be left behind. A depot was accordingly established here, consisting of one regiment of Bengal Infantry, one company of European foot artillery, some heavy ordnance, and some *gikwar*, or native horsemen, the whole under the command of Brigadier-General Nott. This arrangement was reported to have given rise to some angry altercation between the latter officer and Sir John Keane previous to the departure of the commander-in-chief for Kandahar, General Nott being indignant at being thus invalided and debarred his share in the danger and glories of the campaign. We remained at Quetta about a week, the condition of both men and horses being such as to render rest necessary. The supplies which we obtained from the Bengal column and the rich pasturage of the surrounding country soon refreshed and re-invigorated us, and we pursued our route in renewed health and spirits.

Leaving Quetta, we again entered a barren and mountainous district which presented few traces of cultivation, and which afforded little or no pasturage for our cattle. In order to embarrass us the more the Belochees lay on the watch for the parties who were sent out to cut grass, and maimed and mutilated them in the most shocking manner. One poor fellow had his ears slit, and another received injuries which rendered the amputation of an arm necessary. The thefts of cattle, however, became less numerous, the cutting off the supplies of forage being deemed a less hazardous and equally effectual mode of impeding our progress.

So serious became this change in the tactics of the enemy that it was resolved to increase the number of men sent out on the foraging expeditions. This did not, however, deter the Belochees from repeating their attacks, and on one occasion they drove in a party consisting of a considerable number of native soldiers, and succeeded in making three or four of the grass-cutters prisoners. A squadron of Her Majesty's 4th Light Dragoons was immediately ordered out in pursuit under the command of Major Daly. We proceeded towards the hills at full gallop, and at length came in sight of the enemy who were in a close body of from three to four hundred. They suddenly disappeared from view, although the country was still a perfect level, and presented no apparent means of concealment.

On reaching the spot we found they had ensconced themselves in a large stone pit or quarry, into which it was impossible for cavalry to penetrate, and a sharp and well directed fire from all the salient points of the rocks affording the least shelter, indicated to us their different lurking places. Patiently watching our opportunities we sent a volley into every recess or cavity where a rag; was to be seen fluttering, and Major Daly observing a party of about ten or twelve clustered in some bushes which lay almost within a bound of his horse gallantly dashed the animal down the descent, followed by Lieutenant Janvrin, the quartermaster of the regiment, and with a couple of hog spears, which they happened to have with them they dispatched several of the party. The others made their escape by plunging deeper into the recesses of the quarry.

The night now setting in, the Belochees took advantage of the obscurity to steal out of their lair and creep through our lines one by one. They did not get off, however, without further loss. Hearing a rustling noise within a few feet of me, whilst on the watch, I listened attentively and felt convinced that some of them were endeavouring to effect their escape by crawling along the ground on their hands and knees. I plunged my spurs in my horse and clearing the distance at a bound, just as I observed two men rising from the ground, I cut them both down, notwithstanding a most determined resistance, in the course of which they fired twice at me. Several others were disposed of in like manner, but no prisoners were made. We returned to camp about nine o'clock, well satisfied with the issue of our adventure.

The grass cutters who had been made prisoners, and who were abandoned when it was found that our pursuit was likely to prove successful, had received no other injury at the hands of the enemy, than a severe thrashing with a bamboo. The poor fellows were terribly frightened, and felt most grateful for their deliverance.

Major Daly and two privates were severely wounded in this affair. Beside a thrust of a sabre in the chest the major received a musket ball in the left foot, which disabled him for some time from active service. We also found that several of the horses had been injured, it being a favourite trick of the enemy to hamstring them, or rip their bellies open, whenever they could get within reach of the animals.

A treacherous trick played us by one of the neighbouring chiefs, the Khan of Khelat, added in no small degree to the difficulties we had to encounter. The *khan* had promised allegiance to Shah Soojah, and undertook to facilitate the progress of the British troops through his territories. Instead of fulfilling the friendly professions he had made towards us, he interdicted the villagers from bringing supplies to the camp, and cut off almost all the mountain streams. Several of the camp followers who ventured out in search of water, were either carried off or murdered, and our situation became distressing in the extreme. In one day's march of fifteen miles, we left upon our track the bodies of nearly one hundred men, who died from sheer physical exhaustion.

Continuing our progress towards the Khojuck heights, where we expected to meet with determined opposition, we lost a number of men on the route from their own imprudence in venturing at a distance from the camp after dusk. One of them, a Portuguese cook, belonging to my own regiment, lost his way in proceeding to the bazaar for necessaries, and fell into the hands of the Belochees, who were always hanging on our rear. His cries being heard by some soldiers returning from the bazaar, they ran towards the spot from whence the noise proceeded, and were received with a volley of bullets. They did not of course venture farther, being ignorant of the number of the enemy, but on procuring assistance from the camp, they discovered the cook with his throat cut, the head being nearly severed from the shoulders.

Sickness now increased alarmingly amongst us, owing to the bad quality of the attar or flour, as well as the reduction in our usual quantity of rations. The cattle were little better off, and the difficulties of the route increased at almost every step. Water continued as scarce as ever, for the natives filled up or concealed part of the wells and poisoned the remainder. Of the latter fact, we received intimation in time to prevent accidents, and chance befriended us as regarded the former. After a harassing day's march some soldiers of the 17th Infantry, who had set out in search of water, were unsuccessful and were bewailing their hard fate, when the unusual moistness of the place where they had pitched their tent attracted their notice. They sounded the ground and finding it hollow, immediately arrived at the conclusion that it was a well that had been freshly covered over. Further examination confirmed this supposition, and about half an hour's work revealed a deep hole to their sight, in which they found a spring of excellent water. This discovery created such joy and frantic eagerness in the camp that the authorities were obliged to place a strong guard with loaded muskets over it in order to keep back the pressure of the crowds who flocked to it.

In the course of the next day's march we came upon a part of the road which was literally strewn with human skeletons and broken matchlocks. Of the various surmises current amongst us as to the occasion of this wholesale butchery, the most probable was, that one of the caravans travelling to Kandahar had been attacked and overpowered by one of the marauding tribes of the district.

CHAPTER 5

Thief in the Night

We reached the Khojuck Pass in the expectation of finding it occupied by the forces of Dost Mahommed, but contrary to general anticipation it was abandoned. We learned that the Dost had visited the place a few days before, in company with several of his chiefs, when the prudence of disputing our passage was discussed. Owing to some violent differences of opinion amongst the subordinate chiefs, the idea was abandoned, and the enemy fell back towards Kandahar. How different might have been the fate of the expedition but for this impolitic and cowardly step. To enable the reader to judge of its importance a brief description of the pass will be necessary.

Ascending an eminence of no great height a platform of rock is gained, from which a glorious view bursts upon the sight. Immediately beneath is a steep declivity, along whose rugged sides winds the narrow road, while a chasm of immense depth yawns beneath, and threatens to engulf the luckless passenger should he chance to slip as he treads his way down the difficult and dangerous descent. Receding into the far distance lie long ranges of blue mountains broken at intervals into open plains and valleys, whose calm and smiling aspect contrasts well with the frowning majesty of the neighbouring heights.

Nothing could be finer than the view which presented itself as our troops wound round the brow of this tremendous precipice, their arms glittering in the sun, and their uniforms imparting a gay and dazzling variety to the sober hues of the stunted herbage with which its sides were clad. The Infantry, consisting of several companies of the Queen's Royals and a party of the 17th Regiment were ordered to line the heights in order to protect the descent of the artillery and cavalry, together with the heavy baggage. So steep was the road (if road it could be called) that the cavalry were obliged to dismount and lead their horses, bridle in hand, and the artillery to unlimber their guns and drag them down the precipice, a task, as the reader may conceive, of no small labour and difficulty. About half way down, a camel, laden with camp equipage, missed its footing and was precipitated into the abyss with its conductor, and both were of course, immediately dashed to pieces. We reached the plain without any further mishap about six o'clock the same evening, and had every reason to congratulate ourselves that the cowardice or negligence of the enemy had prevented them from disputing our passage.

Having halted at the bottom of the pass two days so as to enable the remainder of the heavy ordnance and baggage to descend we proceeded towards Kandahar. The enemy occasion-ally made their appearance, and though not caring to face us in the field, continued to harass us severely by hanging on our rear, and cutting off the stragglers. Nor did they abate in the least in their love of thieving, robberies being just as frequent, and characterised by as much ingenuity and daring as ever. Late one night I was on sentry before the tent of Lieutenant Kemp when a rustling noise attracted my notice; on looking atten-tively towards the spot from whence it proceeded, I perceived an Afghan crawling towards the tent on his hands and knees, and suffering him to enter, in order the more easily to secure him, I surprised him as he was in the act of plundering it. The fellow was completely naked, and on my attempting to lay hold of him he slipped through my fingers like an eel, owing to the quantity of grease with which his person was smeared, and succeeded in clearing the lines in safety. I did not shoot him because positive orders had been issued against shots being fired in camp, which

45

had before given rise to many groundless alarms.

The weather now became excessively hot, the thermometer being 125 degrees in the shade, which rendered it necessary that we should prosecute our way either in the cool of the morning or at night. The nights were so beautiful that the latter could not be deemed a hardship, and had the scenery been but equal to that through which we had just passed, it could not have been seen to greater advantage than under these clear delicious moonlights. Nothing, however, can be more flat or uninteresting than the country between the Khojuck Pass and Kandahar. The only thing that might be said to have broken the monotony of the route was an occasional shot which told the fate of some poor horse, who, having been broken down by fatigue and privation, and rendered incapable of further exertion, was mercifully put out of pain by its rider. There were nearly fifty head of cattle disposed of in this way between the pass and Kandahar, a pretty item in the expenses of the campaign, when it is borne in mind that each of them had cost from fifty to sixty pounds in India. Had we come in contact with the enemy at Kandahar as we expected, I have no doubt the cavalry would have been found wholly ineffective from the jaded and worn-out condition of their horses.

We arrived at Kandahar on the 4th. of May, and effected a junction with the remainder of the Bengal forces under Sir Willoughby Cotton. Here we were also joined by Shah Soojah in company with Sir William MacNaghten and Sir Alexander Burnes. The dethroned monarch immediately took possession of his ancestral palace, which had just been evacuated by the enemy. The reverses of fortune to which these Asiatic sovereigns arc subject have so steeled them against adversity, that I doubt if his Majesty was agitated, even by a passing emotion, at this important event If he felt at all, it was perhaps more a sensation of fear than joy, for he could not conceal from himself the fact, that the opinions of his subjects were arraigned to a man against him, and that under such circumstances his tenure of sovereignty would in all probability be terminated by a bloody death.

Tired as we were of the harassing mountain warfare in which we had been engaged, and anxious to strike a blow which would decide the fate of the campaign, we were yet agreeably disappointed at the evacuation of Kandahar by the enemy. We were greatly in need of rest after the long and fatiguing marches, which we had made; and the deplorable condition in which we found ourselves, as regarded supplies, rendered it highly impolitic to bring us just then in face of the enemy. Sickness had increased alarmingly amongst us, but in this respect we did not find our position improved, for the excessive heat which prevailed during our stay here carried off great numbers of the men.

Although the bazaar was plentifully supplied with meat and fruit, flour was difficult to le obtained, the stock on hand having been eagerly bought up by the troops on their arrival. The traders turned the scarcity of this necessary article to profitable account, for they only gave 2 lb. to the *rupee* instead of 40 lb., the usual proportion. We had been living on half rations, and these not of the best quality, for nearly a month previous, and had looked forward to our arrival at Kandahar for some addition to the quantity, but so far was this from being the case, that it was found necessary to put the camp followers on the same allowance, and it was not until three weeks after our arrival that an increase and that not the full one, was served out to us.

"We were in daily expectation of the arrival of a convoy of six hundred camels laden with provisions and grain, but intelligence having been brought us that the Afghans lay in way to intercept it, it was thought advisable to send out a force consisting of two squadrons of native cavalry, a party of Her Majesty's 13th Light Infantry and two field pieces for its protection. The enemy being informed by their spies of this movement, fell back to the hills, and the supplies were brought in safety to the camp. The native contractor who furnished them, was offered a bribe of 10,000 *rupees* by Dost Mahommed to direct his camels another way, but much to his credit refused it.

Kandahar is a place of considerable importance in a commercial point of view, but its military advantages are scarcely deserving of notice. It is surrounded by an old wall and ditch, some efforts to strengthen which had been made by throwing up a few parapets, but they were abandoned at the first news of our approach. The principal entrance faces the south and leads directly into the bazaar, which presents rather an animated scene to the eyes of the stranger, in consequence of the varied and picturesque costumes of the multitudes who resort to it, and who are composed of Asiatics of almost every race. The merchandise exposed for sale is no less heterogeneous in its character than its vendors, and much to our surprise and gratification it included good broad-cloths and Whitechapel needles, articles which, in the dilapidated and transparent state of our clothing, proved of no small service to us.

Common and disgusting as mendicancy has become through all parts of Asia, I have never seen it carried to such an annoying extent as here. Our ears were assailed on all sides by whining petitions, and our eyes offended by the exhibition of festering sores or simulated deformities. The ingenuity displayed in twisting a straight and well made limb into some hideous distortion, or in painting up an ugly case of cancer, would have excited the admiration and envy of the importunate cripples who beset the chapels of Catholic countries.

At the further extremity of the bazaar stands a noble mosque, in which are interred the remains of Shah Soojah's father and grandfather. A lofty gilt dome and graceful minarets distinguish it above the other buildings of the town, and the effect, as it is approached from the distance, is extremely imposing. On entering this beautiful temple the visitor is conducted up a flight of marble steps to a platform within the dome, where the remains of the deceased princes lie. The tombs are covered with palls of blue velvet, fringed with gold, and illuminated by about two hundred lamps, which are kept burning night and day, while forty *faquirs*, or priests, watch perpetually over them. Two magnificent folio editions of the Koran, bound in velvet and ornamented with characters of gold, were also shown to us with a degree of reverence that proved the estimation in which they were held. A few pigeons which were flying round the interior of the building appeared to divide with these costly exemplars of the Book of Life the regard and veneration of the votaries of the temple, this bird being held sacred, and any invasion of its privileges visited by the punishment of death.

Several of the Afghan chiefs who were known to be devoted to the interests of Dost Mahommed becoming alarmed at the turn affairs were taking, or, as some said, being dissatisfied with that prince for refusing to guarantee the safety of their women, now came into camp and tendered their allegiance to Shah Soojah. These reluctant auxiliaries were warmly received by the politicals, who hailed their adhesion as an omen of the success of the expedition; and I observed Sir Alexander Burnes carry his joy so far as cordially to embrace one of them. The chief smiled grimly, but said but little. I had an opportunity however of ascertaining his real feelings, on getting amongst his followers a few days afterwards. They openly expressed their regret at being compelled to join the invaders of their country, and stated, that they could not have a braver leader, or a better prince, than Dost Mahommed. They described him as being of a just and generous nature, whilst they represented the *shah* as being cruel and unprincipled.

These Afghan horsemen were a fine athletic set of men, and capitally mounted, their breed of cattle being much superior to ours, and exhibiting proofs of the most careful grooming. The riders wore coats of mail with steel gauntlets, and their arms consisted of a sabre, heavier and longer than ours, a dagger, and in some instances shields and matchlocks. I have no hesitation in saying that the Afghan cavalry, if these were a fair sample of them, are a most effective body of men. They may not be equal to ours in the field, but for a harassing system of mountain warfare where they are required to make sudden descents upon infantry, hemmed in between defiles, and embarrassed by ignorance of the country, no body of troops can be better adapted. Their horses are light limbed, but strong and wiry, and capable of undergoing incredible fatigue while the trooper himself, practised from infancy in the management of the animal, can ride him over places where no European horseman would venture. Had these wild mountaineers but the advantages of discipline and proper organization their country would be inaccessible to any troops in the world.

CHAPTER 6

Towards Ghuznee

In order to give a sort of political *éclat* to the steps taken to reinstate Shah Soojah on the throne of his ancestors, it was resolved that he should be solemnly inaugurated at Kandahar, and nothing was omitted that could possibly tend to render the ceremony imposing. On the morning fixed for its celebration, the whole of the British forces were paraded in review order on a large plain to the north of the city, whilst the *shah's* troops were drawn up at a little distance. In the centre of the field stood a platform canopied with crimson silk, and ornamented with numerous banners and devices, the seat reserved for the *shah* being ascended by a broad flight of tapestried steps, and covered with cushions of crimson and gold. The other accessories of the pageant were got up in similar costly style, but the effect, on the whole, conveyed to the mind rather the unsatisfied feeling which attends the hollow show and glitter of the theatre, than the idea of substantial power.

The weather was beautiful, the sun shedding its gorgeous rays full upon us, and finding innumerable reflections in the military panoply beneath. The heat was however excessive, and the majority of us would have willingly exchanged our places in the ceremonial for the shade and repose of our tents.

As early as six o'clock the commander-in-chief took up his position in front of the line, and was received with a general salute. The *shah* was soon after observed leaving the gates of the city on an elephant, the howdah of which was of solid silver. His Majesty appeared to me to be between fifty and sixty years of age; of middle stature, and somewhat inclined to corpulency. His features were large, but regular, and the expression which played about them was not calculated to leave a favourable impression on the physiognomist. It had a mingled character of vacillation and cruelty about it, which impressed one with the notion that the possessor could sink with ease from the extreme of tyrannical self-will to the abject and fawning humility of the slave.

His Majesty was accompanied by his *vizier*, a tall, spare looking man of a thoughtful and rather melancholy cast of features, and somewhat older than his master. Immediately behind the *shah* rode Sir William MacNaghten, in full court dress, such as is usually worn by officials at her Majesty's levées in England, and he was followed by Sir Alexander Burnes, in a plain suit, and surrounded by the Afghan chiefs, with whom he appeared to be in close and friendly converse. The winning smile and frank and courteous manner of the latter gentleman appeared to have gained for him a degree of consideration amongst the natives, which no other European could boast of, and which was principally attributable to the talismanic influence of qualities that have a never failing effect in softening down and subduing even the most rugged and intractable natures. Nothing could exceed the splendour of the costumes in which these chiefs were clad, their turbans and weapons being studded with diamonds and other precious stones; whilst the horses on which they were mounted were perfect models of animal beauty.

As soon as the *shah* arrived on the ground the bands of the different regiments struck up "God save the King," and his Majesty was conducted to his throne by the politicals. The troops then marched past the platform in slow and quick time each regiment lowering its colours as it arrived before it. A proclamation was afterwards read, declaring and confirming the *shah's* title to the throne, and all persons subject to his authority having been required to yield him fealty, the Afghan chiefs present tendered their homage. The troops were marched back to their lines immediately after, and a Durbar concluded the ceremonies of the day.

It must not be imagined that during all this time our ever watchful enemies had abated their vigilance or lost any opportunity of annoying us. They did not dare to attack the camp itself, precautionary measures having been adopted to prevent their near approach, by stationing inlying and outlying pickets round it. We were compelled, however, to send our camels to graze at some distance from the encampment, and the soldiers in charge of them were frequently surprised and driven in. On one occasion a party of the 13th Light Infantry, consisting of a serjeant and six privates, who had been entrusted with the care of from fifteen to eighteen camels, fell asleep on their posts, being overcome by the excessive heat, and the Afghans, stealing upon them whilst in this state, put one man to death, and severely wounded two others, the whole of the camels of course falling into their hands. The serjeant escaped but was broken for neglect of duty.

Shortly after this occurrence, two of the marauders fell into our hands. In order to put an end to, or diminish these vexatious losses it was determined to make a terrible example of the prisoners, in the hope that it would have some effect upon their companions. They were accordingly tried by a court martial, composed of native officers, and sentenced to be blown from the mouth of a gun. Having been led into the marketplace at Kandahar, they were ordered to draw lots as to who should first undergo this dreadful doom. The younger of the prisoners, a stripling of about nineteen years of age, whose firm and gallant bearing excited universal sympathy and admiration, responded to this command by at once embracing the mouth of the gun from which he was instantly blown to atoms. His companion, a grey-headed man, upwards of sixty years of age, sat looking on, unmoved at this terrible scene, and coolly smoking his *hookah*.

On being ordered to take his place at the gun he did not exhibit the least appearance of fear, and just as the match was about being applied, the officer in command arrested it and directed the prisoner to be taken away, the *shah* influenced, it is said, by the entreaties of Sir Alexander Burnes, having granted his pardon. This unexpected release from the very jaws of death produced as little emotion on the part of this stout old man, as its near approach or the fate of his youthful companion had elicited.

The mysterious and premature death of Cornet Inverarity, of the 16th Lancers, formed, whilst here, the universal topic of discussion in the military circles. The circumstances, as far as I could collect them, were these:—A picnic party had been given by the officers of the regiment at a pleasant rural retreat, within a few miles of Kandahar, and the cornet, being fond of fishing, took his rod and strayed a short distance from his companions in search of sport. His prolonged absence having given rise to remark, some of the party went in search of him, and found the unfortunate gentleman lying dead on the banks of a neighbouring stream. The wounds he had received were of such a nature as to preclude the idea that they were self-inflicted, and there can be but little doubt that he was murdered by the Afghans. The deceased was an officer of considerable acquirements, and was regretted by all who had the honour of his acquaintance. He was only in his 26th year, and had been about five in the service.

I gladly avail myself of the opportunity which presents itself of paying a tribute to the good conduct and friendly feeling of the native troops, who testified on all occasions the utmost willingness, and indeed the most anxious desire to render all the aid and service in their power to their European comrades. Their knowledge of the language of the country, and their acquaintance with the value of its produce, proved of no small advantage to us in our daily traffic with the cunning and thievish traders of the bazaar. Let me add that the general feeling amongst us was that, in privation or danger, we might always count with certainty on the generosity and bravery of the sepoy.

Having passed nearly seven weeks at Kandahar, it was determined that we should next proceed to Ghuznee, where it was reported that Dost Mahommed and his followers had resolved on making a stand. The army quitted the encampment on the 27th of June, preceded by a squadron of European cavalry, two squadrons of the native troops, and two field pieces loaded with canister and grape shot. The route from Kandahar to Ghuznee lies through a wild and mountainous country, and over roads extremely difficult, and at times almost impassable.

The Ghiljies fled on our approach to the numerous mud forts with which these hills abound, and seldom ventured on our track. In the dwellings they had abandoned we found only a few old crones and hungry dogs, both of whom received us with a sort of howling welcome. The Ghiljic huts are constructed somewhat like a bee hive, being of circular and conical form, with interior accommodations of the most wretched description. The few males whom we caught a glimpse of were clad in the same substitute for broad cloth that served the famous Bryan O'Lynn, who having—

"No breeches to wear,
Cut up a sheepskin to make him a pair."

We were lucky enough to discover the stores of corn and *bussorah* (a sort of provender for cattle) which the natives had buried at the first news of our approach. We were also well supplied with water the country being traversed in all directions by rivers and streams. To counterbalance these advantages we were annoyed with shoals of locusts, which literally darkened the atmosphere and kept up a perpetual buzzing and humming in our ears. The locust appears to be a favourite article of food with the natives, who roast it on a slow fire and devour it with eagerness. We could not bring ourselves to relish this equivocal dainty, although our rations were not of the best or most varied description.

As we advanced on Khelat-i-Ghiljie scarcely a day passed without some chief coming into camp from Kabul, with a retinue of from one to two hundred men, in order to tender his allegiance to the *shah*. They were immediately sent to the rear and incorporated with his Majesty's levies. Many of these new auxiliaries brought camel batteries, which created a good deal of curiosity and amusement amongst the European troops, to whom they were a novelty. Each camel carried a sort of rampart on his back, which mounted from four to six swivel guns of small calibre, the conductor both driving the animal and serving the guns. We were surprised at the rapidity and accuracy with which these portable batteries were served and brought to bear, the animal dropping on its knees wherever it became necessary to bring the guns within range, and rising the moment they were discharged.

At Hyder Khail we were plundered of several camels laden with bedding, belonging to Her Majesty's 2nd, or Queen's Royals, and the party In charge of them disappeared and was not again heard of before we left. As we passed Khelat-i-Ghiljie the country began to improve in its character, and large tracts, covered with corn and beans, betokened the presence of a more civilized tribe than that through whose inhospitable territories we had just passed. The villagers came daily into camp with fruit and vegetables, which they parted with at reasonable prices, and their conduct to us on the whole was civil and peaceable.

On the 21st. of July we arrived in sight of Ghuznee, the strength of which we found underrated rather than exaggerated. Ghuznee may be said to form the key to Kabul since it commands the only direct route to that place. The citadel is of great extent, and includes within its precincts, three or four bazaars and several streets. It is surrounded on every side by strong bastions and substantial walls, the whole of which had been recently put in repair, and it mounted nine guns (one a 48 pounder) besides innumerable wall pieces, gingalls, and matchlocks. The principal entrance is at the North side, on the road to Kabul, and is approached by a bridge of slight construction, thrown across a deep ditch or moat. To the right and left stretch long chains of lofty hills, which approach the walls so closely on the North side, as to command a view of the interior of the citadel. The enemy, sensible of the importance of these heights, had lined them with troops in order to prevent our planting batteries on them

At the distance of about three quarters of a mile from the fort, and situated in an amphitheatre of hills, lies the town of Ghuznee, which consists of only a few narrow, straggling streets. A narrow, but deep and rapid river, whose banks are studded with rich corn fields, winds its devious route through the pleasant valley in which the town is situate, and half encircles its walls. Nearly equidistant from the town and the fort, and surrounded by luxuriant orchards and vineyards, stands the famous tomb of Mahommed of Ghuznee. It consists of an oblong building thirty-six foot by eighteen, and about thirty feet in height, and is crowned by a mud cupola. The gates are said to be of sandalwood, and were taken from the temple of Somnath by the conqueror, whose remains lie entombed here. The grave stone in the interior is made of the finest white marble, but its once rich sculpture is now nearly defaced, and it presents but few traces of the Arabic characters with which it was formerly inscribed. Over the last resting place of the hero, and in a sadly decayed state, are suspended the banner of green silk, and the enormous mace which he had so often borne in battle.

In the plain to the south of the hills stand two pillars, or obelisks, of brickwork, about one hundred feet in height, and twelve in diameter at the base, which are said to have marked the limits of the bazaar of ancient Ghuznee, and which at present form serve only as conspicuous landmarks for the traveller.

CHAPTER 7

The Fall of the Citadel

We debouched on the plain in front of the fort about eight o'clock in the morning, and advanced upon it in three columns—the cavalry on the right, the artillery in the centre, and the infantry on the left. The commander-in-chief determined to reconnoitre the place in force, and make the enemy show their strength.

On approaching the orchards and walled gardens before described, we found them occupied by the enemy, and the 1st Brigade having been immediately thrown into them, drove the Afghans out of the enclosures in capital style, and forced them to take shelter behind the defences, with a comparatively trifling loss on our side. Our guns were now brought to bear upon the fortress, which had kept up a sharp fire on us from the moment of our appearance, but owing to our having left our heavy battering train behind us at Kandahar we did but little or no damage. About eleven o'clock we drew off, and pitched our camp out of range of the fire of the foot. On our skirmishers retiring from the gardens they were immediately occupied by the enemy, who commenced cheering our retreating parties, in the conviction that they had obtained a victory. Under this impression they instantly sent off expresses to Kabul, to announce the fact, and state that if the whole of the surrounding country could be raised, they had little doubt of being able to cut us off to a man. The garrison spent the night in rejoicings, and blue lights were constantly sent up as signals to their friends on the neighbouring hills.

Next morning the *shah's* camp was threatened on the left by large bodies of horse and foot who were driven off by the cavalry and some of his Highness's troops; whilst another force, consisting chiefly of horse, under the command of one of Dost Mahommed's sons; and at a short distance from him a Ghiljie chief, with about fifteen hundred cavalry, who had hung upon our flank all the way from Khelat-i-Ghiljie, menaced us to the right. This determined the commander-in-chief to expedite matters, and the engineers having made a careful inspection of the fortress, he resolved on carrying it by storm. The whole of the 22nd was consumed in making the necessary preparations, the field hospital being got ready while strong detachments of cavalry scoured the country around, in order to keep the enemy from our lines.

In order to give my readers a correct idea of the strength of the fortifications, and the difficulties overcome by the intelligence and courage of the officers and men of the British army, I cannot do better than to copy the official reports made by the principal engineer officers on the subject. They contain a full detail of the operations up to the moment when the citadel fell into our possession.

MEMORANDUM OF THE ENGINEERS' OPERATIONS BEFORE GHUZNEE, IN JULY, 1839, BY CAPTAIN GEORGE THOMPSON, BENGAL ENGINEERS, CHIEF ENGINEER ARMY OF THE INDUS.

The accounts of the fortress of Ghuznee received from those who had seen it, were such as to induce his Excellency the commander-in-chief to leave in Kandahar the very small battering train then with the army, there being a scarcity of transport cattle. The place was described as very weak, and completely commanded from a range of hills to the north.

When we came before it on the morning of the 21st of July we were very much surprised to find a rampart, in good repair, built on a scarped mound about thirty-five feet high, flanked by numerous towers, and surrounded by a *fausse-braye* and wet ditch. The irregular figure of the enceinte gave a good flanking fire, whilst the height of the citadel covered the interior from the commanding fire of the hills to the north, rendering it nugatory. In addition to this, the towers, at the angles, had been enlarged, screen walls had been built before the gates, the ditch cleared out and filled with water, stated to be unfordable, and an outwork built on the right bank of the river so as to command the bed of it.

The garrison was variously stated from three to four thousand strong, including five hundred cavalry, and from subsequent information we found that it had not been overrated.

On the approach of the army, a fire of artillery was opened from the body of the place, and of musketry from the neighbouring gardens. A detachment of infantry cleared the latter, and the former was silenced for a short time by shrapnel from the horse artillery, but the fire from the new outwork on the bank of the river was in no way checked. A nearer view of the works was, however, obtained from the gardens which had been cleared. This was not at all satisfactory. The works were evidently much stronger than we had been led to expect, and such as our army could not venture to attack in a regular manner. We had no battering train, and to besiege Ghuznee in form, a much larger one would be required than the army ever possessed. The great command of the parapets from sixty to seventy feet, with the wet ditch, was insurmountable obstacles to an attack, either by mining or escalading.

It therefore became necessary to examine closely the whole contour of the place, to discover if any other mode of attack could be adopted. The engineers, with an escort, went round the works, approaching as near as they could find cover. The garrison were on the alert, and kept up a hot and well regulated fire upon the officers whenever they were obliged to show themselves. However, by keeping the Infantry beyond musket range, and the cavalry at a still greater distance, only one man was killed, and another wounded; the former being hit by men sent out of the place to drive off the reconnoitring party.

The fortifications were found equally strong, all round, the only tangible point observed being the Kabul gateway, which offered the following advantages for a *coup-de-main*. The road to the gate was clear, the bridge over the ditch unbroken, there were good positions for the artillery within three hundred yards of the walls on both sides of the road, and we had information that the gateway was not built up, a reinforcement from Kabul being expected.

The result of this reconnaissance was a report to His Excellency the commander-in-chief, that if he decided upon the immediate attack on Ghuznee, the only feasible mode of proceeding, and the only one which held out a prospect of success was a dash at the Kabul gateway, blowing the gate open by bags of powder.

His Excellency decided upon the attempt, the camp was moved that evening to the Kabul road, and the next morning, the 22nd, Sir John Keane in person reconnoitred the proposed point of attack, approved of the plan, and gave orders for its execution. Preparations were made accordingly, positions for the artillery were carefully examined, which excited the jealousy of the garrison, who opened a smart fire upon the party.

It was arranged that an explosion party, consisting of three officers of engineers, Captain Peat, Lieutenants Durand and McLeod, three serjeants, and eighteen men of the sappers in working dresses, carrying 300 lbs. of powder in twelve sand bags, with a hose seventy-two feet long, should be ready to move down to the gateway at daybreak.

At midnight the first battery left camp, followed by the other four, at intervals of half an hour. Those to the right of the road were conducted to their positions by Lieutenant Stuart, those to the left by Lieutenant Anderson. The ground for the guns was prepared by the Sappers and Pioneers, taking advantage of the irregularities of the ground to the right, and of some old garden walls to the left.

The artillery was all in position, and ready by 3 a m. of the 23rd, and shortly after, at the first dawn, the party under Captain Peat moved down to the gateway, accompanied by six men of Her Majesty's 13th Light Infantry, without their belts, and supported by a detachment of the same regiment, which extended to the right and left of the road; when they arrived at the ditch, taking advantage of what cover they could find, and endeavouring to keep down the fire from the ramparts, which became heavy on the approach of the party, though it had been remarkably slack during the previous operations; blue lights were shown, which rendered surrounding objects distinctly visible, but luckily they were buried on the top of the parapet instead of being thrown into the passage below.

The explosion party marched steadily on, headed by Lieutenant Durand; the powder was placed, the hose laid, the train fired, and the carrying party had retired to tolerable cover in less than two minutes. The artillery opened when the blue lights appeared, and the musketry from the covering party at the same time. So quickly was the operation performed, and so little was the enemy aware of the nature of it, that not a man of the party was hurt.

As soon as the explosion took place, Captain Peat, although hurt by the concussion, his anxiety preventing him from keeping sufficiently under cover, ran up to the gate, accompanied by a small party of Her Majesty's 13th Light Infantry, and ascertained that it was completely destroyed. There was some delay in getting a bugler to sound at the advance, the signal agreed on for the assaulting column to push on, and this was the only mistake in the operation.

The assaulting column, consisting of four European Regiments Her Majesty's 2nd Regiment, Bengal European regiment, Her Majesty's 13th Light Infantry, and Her Majesty's 17th Regiment) commanded by Brigadier Sale, the advance under Lieutenant Colonel Dennie, accompanied by Lieutenant Sturt, engineers, moved steadily through the gateway, through a passage inside the gateway, in a domed building, in which the opening on one side rendered everything very obscure, and making it difficult to find the outlet into the town. They I met with little opposition; but the party of the enemy seeing a peak in the column, owing to the difficulty in scrambling over the rubbish in the gateway, made a rush, sword in hand, and cut down a good many men, wounding the brigadier and several other officers. These swordsmen were repulsed, and there was no more regular opposition; the surprise and alarm of the Governor and *Sirdars* being so great when they saw the column occupying the open space inside the gate, and firing upon them, that they fled, accompanied by their men, even the garrison of the citadel following their example. Parties of the Afghans took refuge in the houses, firing on the column as it made its way through the streets, and a good deal of desultory fighting took place in consequence, by which some loss was sustained. The citadel was occupied as soon as daylight showed that it had been abandoned by the enemy, and the whole of the works were in our possession before 5 a. m.

We lost seventeen men, six European and eleven natives killed—eighteen officers, and one hundred and seventeen Europeans, and thirty natives wounded—total one hundred and eighty-two. Of the Afghans more than five hundred and fourteen were killed in the town, that number of bodies having been buried, and about one thousand outside by the cavalry, one thousand six hundred prisoners were taken, but I have no means of estimating the number of wounded.

There were nine guns of different calibres found in the place, a large quantity of good powder, considerable stores of shot, lead, &e., &c., and a large supply of attar and other provisions.

Geo., Thompson, Capt. Engrs.

Chief Engineer Army of the Indus.

The following report by Captain Peat, of the Bombay Civil Engineers, gives a more detailed account of the operations for blowing up the gate, which, it will be seen, were attended with difficulties of no ordinary nature.

"During the reconnaissance the wall pieces were particularly troublesome. This weapon is almost unknown in our service, but it is a very efficient one, especially in the defence of works, and its use should not be neglected. Every fortified post should be supplied with a proportion of them, and a certain number of men in every regiment practised in firing them.

"The charge recommended by Colonel Pasley, for blowing open gates is from sixty to one hundred and twenty pounds, and this is, doubtless, sufficient in ordinary cases; but in this instance we were apprehensive that the enemy might have taken alarm at our being so much on that side of the place, and in consequence, partially or wholly, built up the gateway. It was afterwards found that some attempts of the kind had been made by propping up the gate with beams.

"The charge was so heavy, that it not only destroyed the gate, but brought down a considerable portion of the roof of the square building in which it was placed, which proved a very considerable obstacle to the assaulting column, and the concussion acted as far as the tower, under which an officer's party of Her Majesty's 13th Regiment were standing at the time, but without occasioning any casualties. In cases of this nature it is of course the first object to guard against any chance of failure; and it is impossible, even now, to say how much the charge might have been reduced with safety.

"The enemy appeared so much on the alert, and the *faussebraye* was so much in advance of the gate that we never contemplated being able to effect our object by surprise. The only question was, whether it ought to be done by day or night. It was argued in favour of the former, that the artillery would be able to make so much more correct practice that the defences would be in a considerable degree destroyed, and the fire so completely kept under as to enable the explosion party to advance with but little loss, and with the advantage of being able to see exactly what they were about. Captain Thompson, however, adhered to the latter, and we were afterwards convinced it was the most judicious plan; for although the fire of the artillery was necessarily more general than it would have been in daylight, still it was so well directed as to take up a good deal of the attention of the besieged, and draw upon their batteries a portion of the fire, which in daylight would have been thrown down upon the explosion party and assaulting columns.

"It would also, even in daylight, have been difficult, with our Light Artillery, to have kept down the fire so completely but that a few matchlock men might have kept their position near the gateway; and in that narrow space a smart fire from a few pieces might have obliged the party to retire. The obscurity of the night, to say nothing of the confusion which it must occasion among undisciplined troops, is certainly the best protection to a body of men engaged in an enterprise of this nature. Blue lights certainly render objects distinctly visible, but their light is glaring and uncertain, especially to men firing through loopholes.

"The party consisted of eighteen officers, twenty-eight sergeants, seven buglers, and two hundred and seventy-six rank and file. It was made of this strength, not only to keep up a heavy fire upon the parapets, and thereby divert attention from the party at the gateway, but also because we were not aware whether the *fausse-braye* was occupied or not, and as it extends so much in advance as to take the gate completely in reverse, it would have been necessary, had a fire opened from it, to have carried it by assault before the party with the bags could have advanced. The party with Lieutenant Durand was accompanied by six men of the 13th, without their belts, the better to secure them from observation, to protect them from any sortie that might be made from the postern of the *fausse-braye* on the right, or even from the gate itself, while another party under an officer, Lieutenant Jennings, accompanied me as far as the tower so as to check any attempts that might have been made from the *fausse-braye* on the left, and at the same time keeping up a fire on such of the enemy as showed their heads above the parapet; of this party one man was killed and a few wounded.

"Nothing could have been more gallant than the conduct of Lieutenants Durand and McLeod, and the men under their command; or more efficient than the manner in which they executed their duty.

"The powder being in sand bags of a very coarse open texture, a long hose and port fire was thought to be the safest method of firing it. The end of the hose fortunately just reached the small postern. The casualties, however, during this operation were much fewer than was expected, being in all one private killed, two sergeants, and twenty-three rank and file wounded.

"The heaviest fire was certainly outside the bridge, for the enemy near the gateway being marked, whenever they attempted to shew their heads above the parapet, were obliged to confine themselves to the loop-holes, the range from which is very uncertain and limited against men moving about. A high loopholed wall, although imposing in appearance, is a profile but ill adapted to resist attacks of this nature.

"The enemy were perfectly aware that we were in the gateway, but appeared to have no idea of the nature of our operations. Had they been so they might easily have rendered it impossible to place the powder bags, by throwing over blue lights, of which they had a large quantity in store. The powder pots and other fireworks so much used by the natives of Hindostan would certainly have rendered the confined space leading to the gate much too hot for such an operation; but the ignorance of the besieged was known and calculated upon, the result shows how justly.

"Their attempts at resistance were confined to the fire from the loopholes and throwing over large pieces of earth, some of which appeared to be intended to knock off the port fire.

"I on this occasion received an excellent lesson on the necessity of not allowing preconceived opinions to lead to any carelessness, in accurately ascertaining the result of any operation of this nature. The gateway appeared, from what I had seen from the hills to the north, to lead straight into the town, and on running in to examine it after the explosion I was so much impressed with this idea and so much convinced of the probability of the gateway having been blocked up during the day, that I was led to believe that it had actually been done, from seeing, in front of the gate that had been destroyed, the outline of an arch filled up with brick masonry. The true entrance turned to the right and would have been discovered by advancing a few paces, and that in perfect safety, for the interior was secure from all fire. Lieutenant Durand on first going up saw from through the chinks of the gate that there was a light and a guard immediately behind it, and from that circumstance was convinced that no interior obstacles of importance existed.

"My mistake therefore was luckily immediately corrected without any bad consequence resulting.

"A party of sappers with felling axes, and commanded by Lieutenant Wemyss, and two scaling ladders in charge of Lieutenant Pigan, accompanied the assaulting column.

"Of ten engineer officers engaged in this attack, only one, Lieutenant Harriot, was slightly wounded. Captain Thompson however had a very narrow escape, having been thrown down by a rush of some swordsmen into the gateway, and nearly sabred while upon the ground."

CHAPTER 8

Incidents of the Battles

The cavalry taking no part in these operations I was an idle, but not the less an anxious spectator of the scene. I had never before witnessed effects so awfully grand, or so intensely exciting in their nature as those which immediately preceded and followed the explosion at the gates. The atmosphere was illuminated by sudden and powerful flashes of various coloured light which exposed the walls and bastions of the fortress to view, and revealed the dusky figures of the garrison, in the act of pointing their guns, or endeavouring to penetrate the denseness of the obscurity beneath, in order to assure themselves of the position of their assailants. Then followed the din and roar of artillery—the terrific explosion of the gates—the crash of woodwork and masonry— the hollow rumbling of the old towers as they came in huge masses to the ground—the rush of the storming party through the breach, and the deafening cheers and shouts of besiegers and besieged.

It seemed as if all the elements of destruction had been let loose at once, and yet I panted to be in the midst of them. I hardly dared to breathe from the very intenseness of my anxiety, and it was not till I saw the British flag floating from the citadel, that I could respire freely. To the soldier there is nothing more trying or chafing than to be condemned to a state of inaction during the progress of such spirit-stirring events as these.

While the Afghans were disputing our entrance into the citadel an incident occurred, which for a moment diverted the attention of the combatants and turned their fury into pity. Amongst the foremost of the party who signalised themselves by their desperate gallantry was an aged chieftain, the richness of whose costume excited general attention, his turban and weapons being resplendent with jewels. The hope of plunder immediately marked him out as an object of attack, and numbers at once assailed him. He defended himself like a man who knew there was no chance of life, but who was resolved to sell it as dearly as he could. He had killed several of the Queen's Royals and severely wounded Captain Robinson, when a grenadier of the company to which the latter belonged, seeing his officer in danger, rushed to his assistance, and with a thrust of his bayonet brought the gallant old chieftain to the ground.

The grenadier was about to despatch him, when a beautiful girl, about seventeen, threw herself into the *mêlée* and plunged a dagger in his breast. She then cast herself on the body of the chieftain, for the purpose of protecting it, and the Afghans, forming a sort of rampart before them, maintained their ground until the heroic girl succeeded in getting it conveyed into the interior of the citadel. Shortly after the place was taken she was found weeping over the remains of the brave old man, who, on enquiry, we learned was her father. She was treated with the utmost respect and tenderness by our men, who neither obtruded themselves on her grief nor offered any interruption to the preparations which she made for his interment.

Amongst the prisoners who fell into our hands was Hyder Khan, a son of Dost Mahommed, and late commandant of the fortress. This chief was discovered hiding in a privy by a soldier of the Queen's Royals, who would have bayoneted him but for the timely interference of one of his officers, who chanced to be near the spot. The Afghan leader was immediately brought before Sir John Keane, and the *shah* being present rated him soundly for his treachery. He replied only by a haughty look of defiance, and was consigned to a tent closely guarded by sepoys. The sword found upon this chief, and which is at present in the possession of Sir John Keane, was valued at 14,000 *rupees*.

Of the many prisoners we had taken, the capture of none afforded such gratification as that of Ghool Mahommed Khan, to whose bad faith some of our past privations had been owing. This chief had entered into a contract with Sir Alexander Burnes, to establish magazines of provisions and corn at Quetta, for the use of the British troops, and five thousand *rupees* were paid over to him for the purpose.

He purchased up all the corn of the surrounding districts, but instead of fulfilling his agreement he forwarded it to Ghuznee for the use of the garrison, and was amongst the most conspicuous defenders of the fortress. On being brought before the *shah* his Majesty ordered him to be bowstringed, but before the sentence could be carried into effect he managed to escape. His treachery failed in its object, for the greater portion of the flour and grain which he had supplied now fell into our hands. We also found from five to six hundred horses in the stables of the fortress, all of which were in excellent condition, and ranging in value from seventy to a hundred pounds each.

I entered the fort shortly after it surrendered and at every step spectacles of the most shocking and revolting nature met the eye. Round a long twenty pounder, which was planted to the right of the entrance, lay heaps of dead Afghans, who appeared to have attached the greatest importance to the service of this piece from the numbers who crowded to perform the duty whenever our fire killed those engaged in it. The agonising cries and groans of the wounded wretches who lay stretched at every side, and who craved drink to sate their burning thirst, struck those who had not been engaged in the fearful excitement of the scene with horror and pity, whilst at every turning a horse, wild with the injuries he had received, was to be met galloping furiously along the narrow streets, and treading the bodies of the dying and dead under foot.

Advancing through the bazaar, my attention was drawn towards a venerable looking Afghan, who was seated on the ground with his back propped against a wall, and whose richly ornamented muslin robes were stained with blood, which flowed profusely from a wound in his breast. A fine looking youth of about fourteen years of age was attempting to staunch it, and I hastened to proffer my assistance. The old man, however, pushed me back, and would not let me approach him, plainly indicating by his gestures that he held me and my countrymen in abhorrence.

Whilst standing at a short distance from him, a straggling ball came whizzing past me, whether intentionally or accidentally I cannot say, and put an end to his sufferings. Some soldiers, who afterwards examined the person of this old chief, for such from his attire I took him to be, discovered amongst other things an extremely well executed map, on which the whole of the route of our troops from the point at which we had disembarked to our arrival at Ghuznee was plainly indicated.

Some of the Afghan women were occasionally to be met turning over the bodies of the dead, in the hope of being able to discover their relations or friends, and giving way to their grief in the most heart-rending lamentations. They were the most superior class of women I had as yet seen amongst the Asiatics, their features being regular, and finely formed, and their eyes piercing, but at the same time soft in their expression. Although nothing like violence was used towards them, they did not escape some incivilities at the hands of our men, owing to the fact that a number of Afghan soldiers had attempted to escape in female disguise.

Various were the adventures related amongst us, as having occurred on the first entrance of our troops into the fortress. A Scotchman, belonging to my own regiment, named James Hamilton, who was known to be an inveterate snuff-taker was discovered in a tobacconist's shop in the bazaar literally covered from head to foot with the contents of the *chatties* or jars with which it was filled, and testing the qualities of each with an air of the most exquisite relish, his nose having been long a stranger to its favourite aliment.

The ruling passion was exemplified in different ways in oth–

ers. Some sought for drink, of which there was little to be obtained and others for gold, which we had every reason to believe was plentiful, if we knew but where to find it. A soldier of the 13th Light Infantry, more fortunate than his fellows, lit unexpectedly on a jar which was filled to the brim with gold pieces to the value it is said of £600 sterling, and conveyed it secretly to the camp. Becoming apprehensive that this large sum would be discovered on him, and that he would be obliged to give it up to the prize agent, he distributed it amongst several of his comrades in order that they might take care of it. The possession of so much wealth turning the heads of his trustees they thought they might allow themselves a few indulgences at his expense, but their excesses ultimately betrayed the secret and they were compelled to hand over the money to the common fund.

As the soldiers severally left the fortress to return to the camp they were stripped of the plunder which they had obtained, and a goodly heap of armour and weapons of every kind was soon piled before the entrance. Amongst the number of curious articles obtained in this way was an old shield, which had belonged to one of the Afghan chiefs and which, though remarkable for the oddness of its construction, presented little else to attract the eye. Its material appeared to be a compound of copper and some white metal, and it was thrown aside by the prize agent amongst the most valueless of the objects which fell under his care.

A soldier of the Bengal European regiment, who had been a jeweller by trade, happened to observe the circumstance, and carelessly taking up the shield, as if to examine the devices with which it was ornamented, scrutinized it for some time, and went away without making the slightest observation. He immediately repaired to the captain of his company, and told him to bid for the shield at the prize sale which was to take place a few days afterwards, advising him not to stop at any reasonable price for it. The officer acted on the hint, and obtained the article for about thirty or forty *rupees*. The shield turned out to be of the purest and finest gold, and the fortunate possessor felt so grateful to his informant that he made him a present sufficient to purchase his discharge, and carry him home to England.

Amongst the different ensigns captured from the enemy on this occasion were two banners of green and crimson silk, trimmed with gold lace and inscribed with precepts from the Koran. They were desperately defended, the Afghans appearing to attach great importance to their safety. They are, I believe, at present in the possession of Her Majesty's 17th Light Infantry, and the Bengal European Regiment. Shortly after the breach had been effected intelligence was brought to the commander-in chief, that numbers of the enemy were making their escape through one of the back gates. He immediately dispatched the 1st Bombay Light Cavalry in pursuit. The Afghans being daring horsemen, and better mounted than our men, made at once for the hills, where they knew our cavalry could not follow.

Aware of this our men put their horses to their utmost speed, in order to intercept them before they got entangled in the de-files. The chase soon assumed a character of lively interest. An Afghan, worse mounted, or less skilled in horsemanship then his fellows, was overtaken and cut down, and the pursuers pressed hard on the heels of another. The cheers of his enemies, and the clatter of their horses' hoofs sounding fearfully near in the ears of the pursued he put the noble animal on which he was mounted to its utmost speed, and cleared the space between him and his companions at a bound rather than a gallop. Again he was almost within reach of the sabres of our men, and again did the fleetness of his horse place him for a time in safety. As he was about to plunge into a deep ravine after the other fugitives a shot brought his horse upon its knees, and the rider was flung upon his head. All now seemed over with him. Starting, how-ever, to his feet, he turned upon his pursuers, and single handed opposed a host of them. Warding off the blows which rained on him from every side, he kept rapidly retreating until he gained the brow of a steep declivity over which he flung himself and was instantly lost to view.

Disappointed in their pursuit, our men took an unmanly re-venge on some peasants who were peaceably engaged in agricultural occupations near the spot. One of these wanton acts of cruelty met with a just retribution. A *havildar* or serjeant, seeing a young Afghan following the plough at a little distance, galloped up, and made several cuts at him with his sabre. The young man ran to the other side of the plough, and placed the serjeant at bay. The latter drew a pistol from his holster, and was about to shoot him, when his horse stumbled over the plough and fell on his side, breaking the leg of the havildar and pinning him at the same time firmly to the ground. The Afghan seized the sword which had fallen from his grasp, and dealt him a blow on the head which instantly killed him. The comrades of the dead man riding up surrounded and captured the peasant, and he was brought into camp to abide the decision of the commander-in-chief. A representation having been made to Sir John Keane of the wanton and unprovoked attack which had been made upon the prisoner, he immediately ordered him to be liberated. The *havildar* was interred on the spot where he fell and there were few in the army who pitied or regretted him.

CHAPTER 9

Dost Mohammed Flees

A few days after the taking of Ghuznee a tragical scene occurred, which pretty clearly indicated how the tide of popular
feeling ran with regard to the restored monarch. There is a poet-
ical superstition that approaching events are often foreshadowed,
and the circumstance to which I allude seemed to impress every
man's mind at the time with the result that has since happened.

The majority of the prisoners who fell into our hands were
released on condition of their serving in the *shah's* army, but
there remained about thirty who refused to accept of their
liberty on such terms. They consisted for the most part of the
immediate followers of Dost Mahommed's father-in-law, and
were devotedly attached to that prince. The *shah*, on learning
the circumstance ordered them to be brought before him, and
expostulated with them on the folly of their conduct. A chief
of haughty bearing stepped from amongst the prisoners, and
after overwhelming His Majesty with reproaches, told him that
nothing should induce him to enter the service of a man who
had brought the horrors of foreign invasion on his country.
Then suddenly snatching a dagger from one of the attendants,
he rushed with uplifted arm towards the *shah*, and would have
pierced him to the heart had not one of His Majesty's servants
interposed his person, and received the blow intended for his
master.

The faithful domestic fell dead at the feet of the *shah*, and the officers and attendants instantly rushed towards the assassin with drawn swords; but he had already anticipated their intention by plunging the poniard in his breast. The *shah*, alarmed and exasperated, ordered the whole of the prisoners to be immediately executed, and in a few minutes their heads were rolling in the dust. This terrible scene created great alarm in the camp, it being at first reported that His Majesty had been assassinated, but the apprehensions to which it gave rise were soon dispelled, by his publicly making his appearance amongst us.

A chief, named Walla Mahommed, who had persisted in firing on the troops several hours after the taking of the fort, and in spite of repeated summonses to surrender, was brought to a court martial by order of the commander-in chief, and sentenced to be shot within the walls of the fortress. He had killed three or four of our men, and wounded one of the native officers by his obstinate folly. He met his fate with the most perfect indifference, for the fear of death cannot be said to be one of the weaknesses of the Afghan character.

I one day paid a visit, with some of my comrades, to the hospital where the wounded Afghans had been carried by their friends. It was situated in the old town, and consisted of a mud hut, whose thatched roof was broken in several places, and afforded little or no shelter against the heat of the sun. The interior was as filthy and disgusting as it is possible to conceive. Into a space of about thirty feet by twelve, were crowded from seventy to a hundred patients, who were disabled by wounds of every description, their sufferings being aggravated tenfold, by the intolerable heat and stench of the place. They were attended by two elderly men and a youth about fifteen years of age, who were busily engaged dressing their wounds, whilst a *faquir* was performing certain charms, by which he pretended he could restore them to health.

Pitiable and disgusting as the scene was I could not help laughing at the mummeries of the fellow. He first placed some cow dung in the hand of the sufferer, and holding it in his, saturated it with water and compelled the patient to smell it.

He then wound up the ceremony by repeating some prayers over the fumes of a charcoal pan, the patient repeating after him certain responses which he directed him to make. This done, he covered him up with an old blanket, and ordered him to lay quiet for several hours, when the cure would be complete. Having of course received a consideration for all this trouble, he left his patients to the progress of the charm, and the discovery, when too late, that they had been grossly duped.

Happening to have a quantity of apples with me which I had just plucked from one of the orchards in the vicinity, I offered them to the sufferers in the hope that they would in some degree refresh them. They accepted them with eagerness which induced some sepoys who were with me to follow my example. The Afghans indignantly refused to receive anything at their hands, and so great was their hatred of the native troops, that they actually spat upon the men who showed them this kindness. Early in August we resumed our march towards Kabul, leaving the whole of our sick and wounded in garrison at Ghuznee.

It was reported that Dost Mahommed intended to dispute every inch of ground to the capital, but these valiant resolutions were abandoned as soon as formed. The only indication of a preconcerted plan of defence which we met with on the route, was a battery of sixteen field pieces which we found planted on an eminence commanding the entrance to a formidable pass about midway between Ghuznee and Kabul, but which had been deserted by the enemy as soon as our advanced columns made their appearance. A party of the horse artillery having been sent to secure the guns and ammunition, an accident took place which was attended with fatal consequences. One of the men having approached a tumbrel with a lighted pipe a spark fell into it and the whole blew up with a tremendous explosion, killing two of the party and severely injuring another.

The conduct of the inhabitants of the different villages along this route, whether influenced by good will or fear, I cannot take upon myself to say, was friendly and well disposed towards us. This did not however prevent some excesses on the part of the native troops, which Sir John Keane sought to repress by issuing an order forbidding the men from robbing the villagers on pain of death. At Chesgow, about two days march from Ghuznee, a soldier belonging to the 2nd Bengal Light Cavalry was observed thieving in the immediate vicinity of the staff lines, and one of Sir John's *aides de camps* who watched his proceedings took a gun from his tent and deliberately lodged its contents in his side. The unfortunate man died of the wound, after lingering a few days. The extreme severity of the punishment and its informal nature, were bitterly canvassed amongst the native troops, but it nevertheless had the effect of preventing a repetition of the offence.

Early on the morning of the 7th of August, we encamped without opposition under the walls of Kabul, Dost Mahommed and his forces having fled to the hills at the first news of our approach. The commander-in-chief being desirous of securing the person of the usurper, immediately despatched Captain Outram, and Hadji Khan, a chief supposed to be well affected towards Shah Soojah, with a thousand Afghans and a hundred native cavalry in pursuit.

They had not proceeded far from the camp when it became evident to Captain Outram that treachery was secretly at work, the Afghans deserting daily, until their number was diminished to about five hundred. Hadji Khan, to whose guidance the force was entrusted, led it by long and circuitous routes, under pretence that they would thereby more easily intercept the fugitives, and turned a deaf ear to the captain's entreaties that they should proceed directly across the hills. Wherever a rapid movement became necessary, the Afghan managed so that his followers should be delayed on the route, and there was no sort of impediment that craft or ingenuity could suggest that he did not employ to retard the progress of the troops. Captain Outram having no authority to act without the aid of the *khan* was obliged to shut his eyes to these manoeuvres, and succeeded after the most urgent persuasion in inducing the Afghan chief to proceed at once to the hills, with a small detachment.

After traversing the highest parts of the Hindoo Kosh, a chain of mountains, fifteen thousand feet above the level of the sea, and extending as far as Bamean, Captain Outram found that Dost Mahommed had taken refuge in the territories of an independent Uzbeck chieftain then at enmity with the *shah*. Whilst crossing the heights several blue lights were thrown up by the orders of Hadji Khan, which the British had reason to believe were intended to give warning to the enemy. Further pursuit through a difficult and hostile territory became of course out of the question, and the horses being worn out from want of forage and rest, orders were given for the return of the party to Kabul. During the march homeward Hadji Khan contrived to give the British the slip, and made off to the hills, rightly calculating that his equivocal conduct would be severely punished by the *shah*. He was, however, captured before the British left Kabul, and sentenced to imprisonment for life. It was said that the commander-in-chief was dissatisfied with the conduct of Captain Outram in this affair, and that he pointedly passed over his name in the official despatches to mark his displeasure.

As several descriptions of Kabul have been published it will only be necessary for me to give such of its leading features as are essential to the completeness of my narrative. The city lies almost in the centre of a semicircular chain of hills, the valley in which it is situated being watered by a noble river which pursues a serpentine and picturesque route through it, and divides the town in nearly equal parts. The bazaar stands at the base of a lofty mountain, up whose rugged sides straggle rude and irregular fortifications of no great strength or importance. The town itself covers a considerable extent of ground, and the streets are in general regular and well built as compared with the other cities of Asia. Towering high above the other buildings may be observed the mosque and Balar Hissar or palace of the sovereign. The latter is surrounded by beautiful gardens and is entered by a large flagged court-way leading to the principal portal of the edifice. The proportions of the building are on a scale commensurate with royalty, the centre being surmounted by a lofty dome, and the wings of vast extent. The right wing contains the stabling of the *shah* and chambers of the household, and the left is appropriated to the sovereign's own use. The general effect of this building is heavy, and it conveys the idea of a prison rather than a palace.

About half a mile to the right of the palace stands the mosque which contains the remains of the Emperor Baber. This temple is one of the finest I have seen in this part of Asia, being of great architectural beauty and noble proportions. It is entirely composed of richly carved stone-work, and is crowned by a number of graceful spires and minarets. The interior is magnificently ornamented with gilding and sculpture, and the pavement is composed of rich mosaics of various coloured marbles. The tomb containing the remains of the Emperor occupies the centre of the mosque, and is less elaborately ornamented than any other part of it, being composed of plain slabs of white marble on which some extracts from the Koran are inscribed.

The bazaar is of circular form, the streets composing it radiating from an open space in its centre, and presenting a thronged and busy aspect. The principal articles of merchandise which attracted our notice were cashmere shawls of the richest and most expensive patterns, and costly silks of every description. A considerable trade is also carried on in preserved fruits, which find their way from here to the most distant parts of Hindostan. In the fruit market we observed grapes which measured nearly two inches in circumference; peaches, whose rich bloom and luscious quality gratified at once the eye and the palate; and strawberries, such as the hot houses of Europe, and all the inventions of horticultural science could not force into existence. As to apples and pears, fruits prized in the western hemisphere, they were in such abundance and of such low price, that they were only deemed worthy of furnishing food for cattle. Almost all the necessaries of life were in equal profusion, beef fetching only a penny, and mutton two pence the pound. It may be readily imagined that to the tired and half-starved soldier, Kabul appeared almost a second land of promise.

CHAPTER 10

At Kabul

It having been announced that early on the morning of the 8th of August the *shah* would take formal possession of the Balar Hissar, the troops were under arras and in review order at ten o'clock. The commander-in-chief, the politicals, and the whole of the general officers and staff rode up, shortly after, to the tent of His Majesty, at which I happened that morning to be stationed as orderly, and were kept waiting some time. Sir William MacNaghten and Sir Alexander Burnes were at length summoned to the *shah's* presence, and having remained with him a few minutes, they came out and informed the commander-in-chief, it was His Majesty's pleasure that the ceremony should be postponed until three o'clock the same afternoon. The reason assigned for this alteration was understood to be an augury pronounced by His Majesty's priests or soothsayers, that the hour was unpropitious, au opinion in which the troops devoutly concurred, the prospect of broiling for several hours under a meridian sun not being extremely agreeable.

At the appointed hour the troops were again under arms, and salvoes of artillery announced the *shah's* departure from his tent. His Majesty was, as usual, borne on an elephant, the *howdah* of which was of silver, and the caparisons crimson and gold. On each side of him sat Sir William MacNaghten and Sir Alexander Burnes, the former attired in the same court dress which he had worn at Kandahar. His Majesty appeared in excellent health and spirits, and addressed much of his conversation to Sir Alexander Burnes, who seemed to be high in his favour. The *shah's* costume was, as usual, magnificent, his turban being ornamented with a single diamond, whose value was estimated at £100,000. Immediately after came six elephants, containing the ministers and household of the *shah*, and then followed the commander-in-chief, with the whole of the general officers and staff in brilliant uniforms, and decorated with their various orders.

The next feature in the procession, and a ludicrous one it was, was the appearance of two burly-looking fellows, dressed in red and yellow, and wearing conical caps, out of which shot two large horns. We at first supposed they were His Highness's jesters, but instead of that they turned out to be his executioners, functionaries far more essential to the comfort of an Asiatic prince. The *shah's* troops, consisting of two thousand infantry, brought up the rear, our own lining the route along which the procession passed.

On approaching the city his Highness was received with loud acclamations by the populace, who gave expression to their satisfaction in barbarous music and salvoes of small firearms. Many of the houses were decorated with flowers, and the windows were crowded with spectators. At the entrance, and in the courts of the palace, was stationed a body of about 250 horsemen, whose steel armour and splendid horses gave them a martial and imposing appearance. They received us with stern and scowling looks, which plainly indicated that their hearts were not in the ceremony which they were compelled to sanction by their presence. On the *shah's* entrance into the palace he held a *durbar*, at which all the British officers were presented to him, and His Majesty took the opportunity of expressing to them individually and collectively his thanks for the exertions which they had made to replace him on his throne.

We had several reviews of the troops during our stay at Kabul, and on each occasion we were honoured by the *shah's* presence. In order to give his Highness some notion of an English horse race, it was agreed that the officers should get up sweepstakes amongst themselves, which the *shah* no sooner heard of, than he added a splendid gold hilted sword with Damascus blade. This increased the spirit of competition, and the Derby or Oaks was never looked forward to with more eager interest. The place selected for the course was a level plain immediately beyond our lines, and about a mile and a half from the city.

From sixteen to twenty horses belonging to the officers of the different regiments were entered for the sword, and it was resolved that three heats should be run for it, the first six horses of the first heat being privileged to run the second, and the third heat being limited to the first and second horses of the second heat. It was agreed that the sweepstakes, which amounted to a considerable sum, should be divided into three parts, for the different breeds and ages of cattle so as to prolong the sport for three or four days.

Six o'clock in the evening being the time fixed for the commencement of the races, the course became crowded, long before that hour, with anxious spectators, the natives not being amongst the least eager lookers on at this, to them, novel scene. The *shah* took up his position near the winning post, attended by the politicals, and the commander-in-chief, but his Majesty did not appear to take much interest in the sport, and he left the course before it was half over.

The officers rode their own horses and turned out in gay striped jackets and jockey caps; so that but for the dark faces and turbaned heads which every where encountered the eye it would not have been difficult to imagine ourselves suddenly transported to Ascot or Epsom. The word having been given, away started the competitors in high blood and spirits; and as the rider belonging to some particular regiment passed the others in his career, the men composing it enthusiastically cheered and hurraed him, others taking up their shouts as their favourite passed him in turn, this military favouritism imparting to the contest a degree of wild excitement such as I have never witnessed on any similar occasion.

The second heat was still more warmly contested, as, according to the regulations above mentioned only the two foremost horses could be entered for the third. Major Daly of the 4th Light Dragoons, and an officer of the 16th Lancers, whose name I now forget, obtained the precedence, after a hard struggle, the race being a neck and neck one the entire way.

As the two successful officers belonged to different divisions, one to the Bengal and the other to the Bombay Army, the partisanship which before had been only regimental now extended to the two armies, and "Bravo Bengal," "Bravo Bombay," burst at every moment from the eager multitudes assembled, as the riders alternately passed or repassed each other in the final heat.

After a contest in which the competitors themselves almost appeared to feel the influence which pervaded the crowd, and to think that the honour of their respective divisions depended upon their success, Major Daly gained the race by about a neck, and was handed the sword amid the delighted cheers of the Bombay troops and the congratulations of his brother officers. The races continued two days longer, and afforded a pleasant recreation to the men after the fatiguing and harassing duties of the last few months.

Brigadier General Arnold of the army of the Indus, having been long suffering under a liver complaint, breathed his last at Kabul shortly after our arrival there. This officer was distinguished for his qualities as a *bon vivant,* and having laid in a good store of necessaries for the campaign, was the only one almost who fared well amidst the general privations. He kept an excellent table along the route, and an invitation to it, was always regarded as amongst the lucky chances by which fortune signified her favour. Good living could not however protect the general against disease, and he fell ill at Kandahar of a malady which is often said to be the result of it. He was carried from Kandahar to Kabul in a *palankeen*, and took no part whatever in the events which occurred between those places. His remains were interred in the Armenian burial ground, outside the walls of the city, and his effects were publicly sold by auction a few days after.

The general had left Bengal with about eighty camels laden

with baggage and necessaries, of which about five and twenty remained at the time of the sale. His trunks were filled with quantities of plate, a goodly provision of snuff and cigars, and such an immense stock of linen that it occupied two days of the sale. His cooking apparatus was most elaborate and ingen ious, and we could not help wondering at the uses to which the infinite varieties of small and curious articles of which it was composed were devoted. The prices at which these effects were sold will appear incredible to the European reader, but it must be remembered that it was the scarcity, in fact the almost total impossibility of getting them, that enhanced their value. The cigars sold at the rate of about two shillings and six pence each, the snuff at ten shillings an ounce, a few bottles of beer, a liquor of which no other officer in the army possessed a drop, at thirty shillings each, and some choice wines at from three to four pounds the bottle. The other things brought proportionate prices, the shirts fetching from thirty to forty shillings each. The amount realised at this sale must have been enormous.

Prince Timour, the eldest son of Shah Soojah, arrived at Ka- bul early in September, escorted by the troops of Runjeet Singh. We expected to find the Sikhs an undisciplined horde of barbar- ians, but they turned out on the contrary to be nearly as well organized as ourselves, being disciplined by French officers, and marching with the same order and regularity as a European reg- iment. Each division was headed by an excellent military band and officered by the same number of grades as ourselves. The men were in general about the middle height, and not so mus- cular or well formed as the Afghans. They are made, however, of the right material for the soldier, being brave, orderly, and tractable, and though they may be considered in some respects inferior to the European troops, they are in my opinion, equal if not superior, to the sepoys.

A detachment consisting of the 4th Light Dragoons, the 16th Lancers, and Her Majesty's Queen's Royals, under the command of Major-General Sir Thomas Wiltshire, was despatched to re- ceive the prince with fitting honours. He was met at a short distance from the town by the British escort, and conducted to the palace amid salvoes of artillery. The prince was a fine youth about one or two and twenty, with a frank expression of countenance and affable manners. The meeting between him and his royal father was said to be extremely affecting, and the prince was unceasing in his expressions of gratitude to the British for bringing about this happy reunion.

Large supplies of arrack, biscuits, and rice, together with money to pay the troops, having been promised from the Upper Provinces, their arrival was looked forward to with some anxiety in the camp, as we could not leave Kabul without them. Information was at length received that Colonel Herring was on his way through the Punjaub, and after a tedious and harassing journey, in which he had to encounter frequent opposition to his progress from the mountain tribes, he at length reached Hyder Khail within one day's march of Kabul.

Riding out alone next morning, for the purpose of inspecting the country, the colonel was set upon by a body of Afghans and barbarously murdered, his body being plundered of every article of value he had about him, and his horse carried off. His mutilated remains were found in the course of the day by some troopers, who had been sent out in search of him, and brought to Kabul along with the stores, which reached that place in safety the same night. He was interred with military honours in the Armenian burial-ground, on the following day. The deceased had been long in the service, and was a gallant and experienced officer. We heard that his murderers were captured shortly after we left Kabul, and put to a dreadful death, by order of the *shah*.

CHAPTER 11

Reprisals

In order to testify his gratitude towards the British, the *shah* resolved to institute an order of merit, to be called the order of the Doorannee Empire, and to confer its respective grades upon three classes of officers, namely, generals, brigadier generals, and field officers. A *durbar* having been summoned, at which the Ministers of State, the politicals, and a number of British officers were present, a chapter of the order was held, and His Majesty, as Sovereign, invested the commander-in-chief, several general and field officers, and the politicals with the decoration, which consisted of a sort of Maltese cross with a jewel in the centre. His Majesty was also pleased to express his desire that every officer, non-commissioned officer, and private soldier in the army should receive a silver medal, commemorative of the campaign, and for this purpose placed a large sum of money at the disposal of Sir John Keane. The Queen's sanction has been obtained to the measure, but the medal has not as yet been issued.

Leave had been given by the officers in command of the different regiments to men entering the town to carry their side arms, as a protection in case of chance collision with the inhabitants. The facility of obtaining intoxicating liquors rendered this a contingency of not unlikely occurrence, and our men soon got themselves into unpleasant and in some instances dangerous scrapes. On one occasion, a private of the 13th Light Infantry having been drinking rather freely, forced himself into the apartments of the wife of a respectable inhabitant. Proceeding to offer her some violence, her screams alarmed the neighbourhood, and the soldier was soon surrounded by a host of angry husbands and fathers, armed with every description of weapon. He defended himself with his bayonet for some time, contenting himself with merely parrying their blows, and had fought his way into the street, when he was met by several others of the townspeople, who set upon the unfortunate fellow and instantly despatched him. They secreted the body until night-fall, and then threw it outside the walls of the town, where it was discovered next morning.

It having been determined that early in September part of the forces should set out on their return homeward, the choice fell upon Her Majesty's 17th Foot, the 2nd or Queen's Royals, one company of foot artillery, a detachment of the 4th Light Dragoons, the 1st Regiment of Bombay Light Cavalry, and two troops of Bombay horse artillery, the whole under the command of Major General Sir Thomas Wiltshire. It would naturally be supposed that after so long an absence from quarters, we hailed this intimation with something like pleasure, but such was far from being the fact. We had rioted in profusion and luxury, and did not relish the idea of again encountering the privations of the long and dreary route which lay between us and India. Added to this we had seen but little of actual fighting, and the promotions had been consequently few.

Promotion and prize money are the all engrossing subjects of a soldier's ambition, and this speedy return put an end at once to our long cherished hopes. We well knew that the restless and turbulent spirit of the Afghan chiefs would not permit them to remain long in subjection to Shah Soojah, and that there would consequently be more work for the British troops. Regret and envy of our more fortunate comrades were therefore the predominant feelings which pervaded nearly the whole of the departing troops.

We left Kabul on the 14th of September, and arrived at Ghuznee, the scene of our former exploits, after eight days' march, during which nothing worthy of mention occurred. It is astonishing how soon the traces of war disappear, and the living gaps caused by its ravages are filled up. The fortress appeared as perfect in its outline as if the hand of the destroyer had not recently passed over it, new gates having been substituted for those which had been damaged, and the breach immediately above them re-filled with masonry. The inhabitants of the bazaar had resumed their accustomed occupations, and scolded, and chaffered, and jested, and laughed, as if they had neither lost relatives nor friends, nor dabbled through mire freshly reeking with their blood. Familiarity, they say, breeds contempt and blunts the feelings, and the Asiatic, before whose eyes such scenes pass almost daily, thinks of them only as the immutable decrees of fate, which cannot be shunned, and ought not to be repined at.

The sick and wounded, of whom we had left numbers at Ghuznee, had almost all died, and were interred in an open space selected for the purpose outside the walls of the fortress. The last resting-place of our brave fellows is situated at the foot of one of the adjacent mountains, but neither stone nor inscription indicates the spot.

The Bengal regiment of native infantry, whom we found in garrison at Ghuznee on our return, and whom we left after us, appeared to be quite as well reconciled to their quarters as we were at Kabul, although the two places appeared to me vastly different in point of health and comfort. The majority of the inhabitants regarded the troops with a sort of sullen indifference, but the trading classes seemed civil enough. The quantities of fish and game with which the neighbourhood abounded, afforded the officers a ready means of dissipating their time, and we would have been well content to have remained here. Orders were however given that we should pursue our route, and we left Ghuznee on the 25th of September, after a stay of only two or three days.

Instead of diverging to the right towards Kandahar, we took the direct route to Quetta, over the Ghiljie hills. The weather had become intensely cold, and the rivers and streams were covered with ice, several inches in thickness. The Rev. Mr. Pigot, our chaplain, happened to be crossing one of them on a pony, when the ice gave way with his weight, and the worthy clergyman was immersed in the water. The stream was not, however, so deep as to occasion any alarm for his safety, and he was speedily rescued from his embarrassment, with no other inconvenience than being kept shivering several hours in his wet clothes, his baggage being at a considerable distance in ad-wince. The rascally native who preceded us as guide grinned maliciously, and told him that if he had not forgotten to say his prayers setting out the accident would not have happened.

On encamping, at the close of the first day's march, from Ghuznee, some soldiers belonging to the 17th Infantry and Queen's Royals, went out in search of water, and met with a draw well, which proved to be dry. One of them descended in order to examine it more closely, and an exclamation of horror escaped him as he reached the bottom. On his companions enquiring the occasion of it, they learned that he had fallen upon several skeletons, the identity of which with some soldiers we had lost on the route upwards was placed beyond doubt by fragments of military clothing and regimental buttons which lay scattered about. Singular to relate, a lark had built its nest in one of the skulls, and was found innocently reposing with its young in this curious receptacle.

The annoyances to which we had been subjected during our route upwards, from the thieving system of warfare pursued by the Afghans, seemed now at an end. Our road lay through bleak and desolate hills, where only a solitary, and timid mountaineer was occasionally to be seen. Numerous rivers and streams traversed this wild country in every direction, and relieved us from all apprehensions on the score of water. Provisions were also plentiful, as the commissariat had taken care to lay in sufficient supplies, and the only inconvenience which we might be said to have experienced was the severe cold of the nights. The barren nature of the country rendered fuel difficult of obtainment, and the consequence was that numbers of the troops were carried off by dysentery.

The march from Ghuznee to Quetta occupied about five weeks, and we thought we should never reach the end of these long chains of hills. Always ascending and descending heights of no inconsiderable elevation, the horses became regularly knocked up with fatigue, and we were obliged to shoot numbers of them on the way.

In a recess in one of these hills, I one day came upon a singular scene. About nine or ten of the natives were assembled around a dead horse and while part of them were cutting steaks from his haunches, the others were engaged cooking them. Revolting as such a sight is to European stomachs, I have seen the time when, on our march upwards, I could have partaken of these same horse steaks with infinite relish.

A few days before our arrival at Quetta, we requited an atrocious act of treachery, which had been committed towards us by some Ghiljie chiefs, with the punishment it richly merited. About one hundred camel drivers, who had left us at Kandahar, on our way to Kabul, for the purpose of returning homewards, took their route over the hills we were now crossing in order to shorten the journey. They were met by the Ghiljies with professions of friendship, and seduced into a mountain fort under the pretence of hospitality. They had no sooner entered its walls than their throats were all cut, and their bodies flung into deep wells for the purpose of concealing the massacre from the eyes of the British.

Information of the fact having been received, Sir Thomas Wiltshire despatched a Squadron of Her Majesty's' 4th Light Dragoons, two companies of native infantry, and two pieces of artillery to raze the fortress to the ground. The cavalry started at two o'clock in the morning, and after a hard gallop of eighteen miles we arrived in front of the Ghiljie strong hold. It was a small but strongly constructed fortress, situated on the brow of a steep declivity and defended by strong wooden gates. The entrance was commanded by an old iron carronade, and a number of loopholes for the discharge of musketry. Not a living soul was to be seen on the walls, and fearing some artifice, Major Daly, our commanding officer, resolved to suspend operations until the artillery came up. As soon as the latter made its appearance, and the guns were placed in a position to command the fort, Major Daly ordered part of the cavalry to dismount and proceed with loaded carbines to the gate, under cover of their fire. No opposition was, however offered to us, the enemy having fled to the mountains, and the gates were forced open in a few minutes.

The only inhabitants we found in the place were a few women and children, but we discovered quantities of the richest silks and carpets, beside arms and money (consisting principally of silver coins) the fortress being a sort of depot for the booty obtained by these highland marauders.

One of the cavalry having entered a dwelling in search of plunder, was suddenly seized by two or three Ghiljies, who unexpectedly made their appearance through a sort of trap, with which almost every house in the fort was furnished. They placed a bandage over his eyes, and were in the act of passing a rope round his arms, when the timely approach of some of his comrades saved him from being carried off as a prisoner, the enemy disappearing through the trap the moment they heard the noise of their footsteps at the entrance. The troopers would have willingly pursued them, but the depth and darkness of the subterraneous passage convinced them it was something more than a mere cellar, and they knew that if they once got involved in its windings they would be completely at the mercy of the enemy.

It is probable that these passages had outlets without the walls, and that it was through them the enemy made their escape at the first news of our approach, the suddenness and quickness of our movements preventing them from taking their valuables with them. There was also abundance of cattle and grain, of which we brought off large supplies to the camp. Orders having been given to the artillery to blow up the fortress, the women and children were sent out of it, and at five o'clock the same day the walls were breached, so as to render them completely useless, and the houses fired in all directions. After remaining to see that the work of destruction was complete, we quitted the place at three o'clock in the morning, and arrived the same day at the encampment. The enemy were not entirely without their revenge, for, following on our footsteps, and watching us closely, they contrived to carry off the cook, and three camels laden with the cooking utensils of the squadron, a loss which was severely felt, and by some thought ill compensated by the booty we had obtained.

CHAPTER 12

Journey to the Coast

We reached Quetta on the 29th of October, and the army separated into two divisions there, one to proceed by the fortress of Khelat, to punish the *khan* for the treacherous trick which he had played us on our way up, and the other to return homeward through the Bholun Pass. The force destined for military operations against Khelat consisted of Her Majesty's 2nd or Queen's Royals, Her Majesty's 17th Regiment of Foot, the 35th Bengal Native Infantry, one company of foot artillery, one troop of horse artillery, with the Poona Irregular Horse, the whole under the command of Major-General Sir Thomas Wiltshire. As my detachment was not included in this expedition, owing to the fatigued condition of the horses, and the difficulty of procuring forage on the route, I can only describe the storming of Khelat from the reports of those who were present at it.

The fortress of Khelat was very little inferior to Ghuznee in point of strength, being defended by strong breastworks and mounted with large cannon. The garrison consisted of from twelve to fourteen hundred men, and there was abundance of provisions and ammunition in the place. After reconnoitring its position Sir Thomas Wiltshire resolved on carrying it by storm, and the affair was a short but brilliant one. A battery was erected on one of the neighbouring heights, and a well directed fire soon brought the gates down. The stormers then rushed up the causeway under cover of our guns; but before they had reached the gateway, a heavy fire from the loopholes of the fortress killed from twenty to thirty of our troops, amongst whom was Lieutenant Gravatt, who was gallantly leading them on.

A desperate hand to hand fight then ensued, the enemy resisting in dense masses, and disputing every inch of ground; but our men carried all before them, at the point of the bayonet, and drove the enemy into the interior of the fortress, where they were headed by the *khan* himself. The old chieftain fought with desperation and though frequently offered quarter, indignantly refused to accept it. He and the followers by whom he was surrounded were all bayoneted on the spot, and in about four hours the whole of the fortress was in the possession of our troops. In the immediate vicinity of the place where the *khan* was killed, a shocking spectacle presented itself.

His favourite women, about twelve or fourteen in number, lay heaped together in a pool of blood, their throats having been cut by order of the *khan*, to prevent their falling into our hands. A large quantity of treasure, consisting of specie and jewels, was found in the citadel, and had the cavalry been present more would have fallen into the hands of our troops, as the enemy were observed despatching it to the hills, on camels, through one of the back gates, during the heat of the assault. Amongst the various effects which were captured on this occasion were several boxes of arms and accoutrements, which had been plundered from us on our way to Kabul, and a telescope and some books, which had belonged to one of our officers. Cattle and grain were also found in great abundance, and proved of no small service to the division, on its route homeward, through the Gundava Pass. The fortress was completely-dismantled before the departure of the troops, and the chiefs and other prisoners liberated on promising allegiance to the *shah*.

Amongst the residents whom we found at Quetta on our arrival was a Bombay Parsee, who had ventured up to that place with supplies, consisting of tea, sugar, hams, brandy, beer, wines, and other necessaries. To the soldier as well as the officer these articles were a welcome treat, and having plenty of money to purchase them we soon exhausted the stores of the enterprising trader who had reason to congratulate himself on the successful issue of his trip.

The morning previous to our departure a suicide occurred under circumstances which gave rise to the suspicion that the wretched perpetrator of it intended to have preluded it by the crime of murder. A trooper belonging to the horse artillery was placed under arrest for some trifling neglect of duty, and as soon as he was liberated he took a loaded pistol and went directly to the tent of the adjutant of his corps who had fortunately quitted it a few minutes before. The disappointed trooper returned to his lines and immediately blew his own brains out.

We left Quetta on the 1st of November, about nine o'clock at night, taking with us the sick who had been left behind on our way to Kabul, and who were now sufficiently restored to proceed homeward. In consequence of the scarcity of water on the route we were obliged to make a forced march of eight and twenty miles, and reached the entrance to the Bholun Pass at six o'clock the next morning. We entertained a lively recollection of the reception we had met with on our former passage through this defile, and now felt some misgivings that we should not be allowed to retrace our steps without a repetition of the favours which were then so liberally showered upon us. To our great gratification and contentment, however, the Belochees offered us no sort of obstruction, and could they have facilitated our progress through their country, would, I have little doubt, been well inclined to do so. We occasionally caught glimpses of them watching our movements at a respectful distance, but they never ventured within musket shot during the whole of our passage. We lost two or three men from sickness before we cleared the defile, and found it almost impossible to inter them from the stony nature of the strata with which the whole of this district is covered.

Quitting the Bholun we proceeded to Dadur, and thence to Bagh, through a jungle abounding with every sort of game, but more particularly deer and wild boar. The troops made their way with considerable difficulty through the intricacies of this entangled route, the pioneers being in constant requisition to clear a passage for them.

On the 24th of November we arrived at Bagh, a village situated at the Kabul side of the desert, elsewhere described. The place consists of a few miserable huts, surrounded by fields of *joharra*, and containing only one tank of stagnant water. Doctor Forbes, of the 1st Light Cavalry, an officer universally esteemed for his benevolence, hearing that the natives were dying in numbers of the cholera, immediately hastened to the village to tender his services. He was seized by the epidemic, and returned to his quarters in a dying state. The unfortunate gentleman expired in a few hours afterwards, and was interred the same day. Five or six of the European troops were attacked in like manner, and were immediately hurried to the hospital tents, where two of them died, but the others struggled successfully against the disease.

Brigadier Scott, taking alarm at these unequivocal evidences of malaria, gave orders that we should proceed across the desert without a moment's delay, and we accordingly struck our tents at four o'clock the same day, carrying our sick along with us. On reaching the extremity of the desert we found the 1st Regiment of Bombay Grenadiers, with a large convoy of provisions and stores for the use of the army. These supplies should have reached us at the other side of the Bholun, but the escort had been attacked by the cholera on the route, and were obliged to remain stationary until the disease had abated. We found them nearly all convalescent and about to continue their route. We took from them a stock of provisions, and pursued our march.

We arrived at Shikarpoor with a great number of sick who had fallen ill of the epidemic on the way, and it was resolved that we should remain here a few days. Shikarpoor is a large well built town, and contains two fine mosques, several roofed bazaars, and two or three large manufactories. The British resident has a fine house here, the gardens of which are tastefully laid out in the European style. Notwithstanding the clean looking appearance of the town it is far from being healthy, and from ten to twelve of our troops were daily carried off by the cholera during our stay.

Amongst the number was Captain Ogle of the 4th Light Dragoons, who fell a victim to his humanity in visiting the sick of his troop. This lamented gentleman was only in his thirtieth year, and was a great favourite with his corps. He was unfortunately a married man, and had been looking forward with feelings of eager anticipation to his reunion with his family. Being of a buoyant and joyous temperament, his loss was felt severely in the circle of his brother officers; his ready jest and imperturbable good humour rendering him the life and soul of the mess table. Captain Ogle looked upon the private soldier as something more than a mere automaton placed at his disposal, and whilst he had always a due regard for the discipline of the service, he exercised the power entrusted to him with humanity and judgement, the act in which he lost his life being but the last of a countless series of generous and disinterested offices which he was in the habit of performing for those under his command. Few men have left behind them a memory so associated with everything that is valuable and estimable in social and military life.

Leaving Shikarpoor, on the 27th of November, we arrived on the following day at Sukkur Bukkur, a town situated on the banks of the Indus, and having its citadel on a rock in the centre of the river. The cholera rapidly disappeared here; but we sustained another loss in the person of Lieutenant Janvrin, the acting quartermaster of our detachment, who was carried off by the smallpox. On the opposite bank of the river lies Roree, a village remarkable only for its manufactures, which consist principally of silks. Several of us having obtained leave to visit the place, we were strolling through the bazaar, when we observed preparations for a wedding in progress. Taking up a position which enabled us to see what was passing, without obtruding on the parties concerned, we waited patiently until the ceremonies commenced.

At the expiration of about a quarter of an hour the bridegroom made his appearance in front of the house which contained his betrothed, and both in person and attire he was all that a native belle could have desired. He was a fine, muscular looking fellow of about seven or eight and twenty, with handsome features and bold and jaunty air. He was dressed in a loose robe, of spotless white, and without any ornaments or weapons whatsoever. Proceeding directly to the door of the house which contained his *dulcinca* he knocked at it three times with the knuckles of his right hand and once with his left. He then threw himself prostrate on a mat which had been made for the purpose, by the lady's own hands, and there waited her coming forth.

The door presently opened, and a number of musicians immediately struck up a wild and discordant air. A timid and pretty looking maiden, about fourteen years of age, showily dressed in different coloured silks, and ornamented with a nose ring and bangles of pure gold, at length stepped forth, followed by her relatives and friends, who formed themselves into a circle around her. The bridegroom starting to his feet made a formal claim to the hand of his affianced and presented her with a garland of flowers, which she gracefully threw across her shoulders, in token that she accepted him, and then suffered him to embrace her.

Lifting her in his arms he placed her on the back of a donkey, and they went in procession to pay visits of ceremony through the town, the bride distributing sweetmeats to the crowd, as she passed along. The bridegroom showered his favours about in the form of some red powder, which he flung in the faces of all near him, and especially in those of the Europeans, of whom there were a good many present. He half blinded some of us, and conferred as dark a hue as his own upon others—freaks that appeared to give infinite delight and amusement to the natives, but which were not taken in quite as good part by some testy fellows amongst us.

Having arrived at the house of the bridegroom's father, the old gentleman graciously descended, and taking the bride in his arms, bore her into his dwelling. The bridegroom remained a few minutes after them, and flinging some cowries to the musicians and crowd, he made a *salaam* and darted in after his *inamorata*.

We remained at Sukkur about six weeks, in consequence of an order forwarded after us by Sir William MacNaghten, under the apprehension that our services would be again wanted at Kabul. The Indus being navigable up to the town, we had plentiful supplies of provisions and other necessaries at moderate prices, and felt tolerably satisfied with our quarters. As to the probability of our having to return to Kabul, the cavalry felt at ease regarding the rumours which prevailed, for they well knew that the condition of their horses put such a thing completely out of the question. An order at length arrived that the various brigades of the Bombay column should be broken up, and that the troops composing them should return to their respective quarters. Brigadier General Scott, and his *aides de camp,* accordingly left us by one of the first boats which sailed down the Indus for Bombay, and we remained under the command of the officers of our respective regiments.

We passed our time hunting in the jungles, in the vicinity of the camp, or in fishing in the river, both of which proved prolific sources of amusement. I went out several times to chase the wild boar, and on one of these occasions the sport nearly proved fatal to me. Proceeding with two of my comrades, and a native for guide, through a dense and almost impenetrable part of the jungle, we suddenly roused a huge boar, which turned fiercely upon us, and made directly at the nearest of its pursuers, which, as chance would have it, happened to be me. He had me down on the earth in a twinkling, and would have made short work of me had not a well-directed shot from one of my companions struck him right between the eyes, and tumbled him lifeless on the ground. The man to whom I owed my safety exhibited admirable coolness, and self-possession, for the slightest deviation in his aim would have sent the bullet through me instead of the object for which it was intended. It was with the greatest difficulty we contrived to drag our prize into camp, for he weighed no less than from twenty-five to thirty stone, and supplied the troop with pork chops until we were tired of them.

The importance of Sukkur as a military position cannot be exaggerated. It forms the key to Scinde, and the Indus being navigable up to the fortress, its supplies do not depend on season or circumstance. These advantages have not been overlooked, for it has since been retained in the possession of our troops, and will always serve as a *point d'appui* in any future operations we may undertake at that side of the Indus.

After passing nearly six weeks at Sukkur, we took the route to Larkhana along the right bank of the Indus. The road lay, as before, through a jungle, and the occasional glimpses which we caught of the river through the clearances gave a picturesque effect to the scenery. We arrived at Larkhana on the 19th of January, and remained there only one day. Proceeding thence to Sehwan we reached the latter place in about four days, and found a gun boat belonging to the Hon. Company lying at moorings in the river. We left Sehwan on the following day, and taking a farewell of the river Indus we proceeded towards the coast through a wild and deserted district, in which we found neither villages nor inhabitants.

Within one day's march of Kurrachee we found a number of tombs richly sculptured and covered with inscriptions from the Koran, which were said to contain the remains of some of the native princes. There being abundance of excellent water here, and Kurrachee having the reputation of not being extremely healthy, it was determined that we should remained encamped here until the Khelat division formed a junction with us. It was not till the end of February, however, that the Khelat forces made their appearance, having kept us waiting about five weeks, and on the day after their arrival we marched into Kurrachee where we found Her Majesty's 40th Regiment.

Kurrachee is situated on the Coast of Belochistan, and its natural advantages entitle it to the rank of a first rate sea-port town. It possesses a fine harbour, in which a seventy-four gun ship may ride in safety, and which is protected by the batteries

101

of the town, and the guns of a fortress occupying an island about midway between the mainland and the promontory which forms the harbour. On our arrival at Scinde, instructions had been forwarded to Commodore Pepper, by the commander-in-chief, to invest the place, and we accordingly found it in possession of our troops on our return.

The town is large but irregularly built, and is surrounded by walls and bastions, on which we saw some pieces of cannon, but they were of small calibre, and of the worst possible construction. To the north of the town we observed a superb banyan tree, which extended its foliage to such a distance, that it formed a pavilion capable of containing a small stone mosque for the accommodation of a number of *faquirs* or priests. Of the many curious specimens of this class that I have met with in Asia, I have seen none so utterly degraded and isolated from everything like humanity. Their bodies were thickly coated over with ashes and red paint, and their hair clotted with filthy moisture. They were surrounded by every sort of abomination, and howled and whined like a set of wild beasts. That they had not reduced themselves to this savage state merely from fanaticism we had abundant opportunities of discovering, for we saw the inhabitants of Kurrachee daily pouring into the temple with rich presents and offerings, and propitiating their good will by sacrifices of their most precious and valuable effects.

To the left of the Mosque lies a tank, or reservoir, about fifty feet long by thirty broad, in which we saw a number of live alligators, which are carefully fed by the priests, and held in the greatest possible veneration and awe by the deluded votaries who repair there.

The feast of the Mohurrum had commenced a few hours before our arrival, but we were in time to witness the greater part of it. A short description of these singular rites may not be uninteresting to the reader. A hole being dug in the ground to the depth of about six or eight feet, fire is placed in it, and the devotees dance round it, with the most extravagant exclamations and gestures, some dashing square pieces of iron or brass together, to add to the effect. According as one set of dancers becomes fatigued they are replaced by another, and thus the ceremonies are kept up without intermission from sunset to daybreak. When the moon is at its full they march in procession to the water's side, preceded by their *taboots*, a sort of fantastical temple, constructed of bamboo and gilt paper. I have seen one of these temples, at Poona, of such large dimensions that it required an elephant to draw it, and cost no less a sum than a thousand *rupees*. On reaching the water's side the *taboots* are thrown in and allowed to float away with the tide. This concludes the ceremonies and the wearied performers are glad to return to their homes.

On returning towards the lines, from the Mohurrum, we saw a miserable looking wretch squatted at the side of the road, who appeared to be in deep affliction, for he was weeping bitterly and lamenting his hard fate. I addressed him and inquired into the cause of his grief. He told me that he had been induced to become a convert to Christianity by one of the missionaries, and had been thrust out of the pale of social intercourse from the moment the fact became known. He deplored his having yielded to the arguments of the missionary, since they had debarred him from participating in the religious ceremony which had just terminated, its pomp and circumstance having evidently made a deeper impression on his imagination than his conviction. We gave him some relief and passed on, when our attention was again directed to him by one of our companions, who had lingered behind. Several of the natives had surrounded the poor convert, and were spitting upon him, and loading him with the vilest reproaches. We returned to the spot and compelled them to leave him in peace.

Amongst the British whom we found on our arrival at Kurrachee was Mr. Masson, the author of an interesting work on Afghanistan, which has been lately published. This gentleman had been originally a private soldier in the Honourable Company's service, and had risen through various grades to the profitable civil employ which he at present holds. He rendered some important services to the company, for which they awarded him a pension of £100 a-year, and much to his credit he settled the whole of it on his aged mother.

After remaining at Kurrachee about ten days, the order was at length issued for the embarkation of the Cavalry, which was now limited to my own detachment. Upwards of thirty *pattemars* were hired for the voyage, and from twelve to fourteen men, and an equal number of horses, were stowed in each. We had a quick and favourable passage, and arrived at Bombay on the 10th of March, after an absence of nearly eighteen months.

Appendix

From the *Delhi Gazette Extraordinary, October 1*, 1842.

"The Right Hon. the Governor-General of India having with the concurrence of the Supreme Council, directed the assemblage of a British force for service across the Indus, his Lordship deems it proper to publish the following exposition of reasons which have led to this important measure.

"It is a matter of notoriety that the treaties entered into by the British Government in the year 1832 with the *Ameers* of Scinde, the Nawah of Bahawulpore, and Maharaja Runjeet Singh, had for their object, by opening the navigation of the Indus, to facilitate the extension of commerce, and to gain for the British nation in Central Asia that legitimate influence which an interchange of benefits would naturally produce.

"With a view to invite the aid of the *de facto* rulers of Afghanistan to the measures necessary for giving full effect to those treaties, Captain Burnes was deputed, towards the close of the year 1836, on a mission to Dost Mahomed Khan, chief of Kabul: the original objects of that officer's mission were purely of a commercial nature.

"Whilst Captain Burnes, however, was on his journey to Kabul, information was received by the Governor-General that the troops of Dost Mahomed Khan had made a sudden and unprovoked attack on those of our ancient ally, Maharaja Runjeet Singh. It was naturally to be apprehended that his Highness the Maharaja would not be slow to avenge this aggression, and it was to be feared that the flames of war being once kindled in the very regions into which we were endeavouring to extend our commerce, the peaceful and beneficial purposes of the British Government would be altogether frustrated. In order to avert a result so calamitous, the Governor-General resolved on author-ising Captain Burnes to intimate to Dost Mahomed Khan, that if he should evince a disposition to come to just and reasonable terms with the Maharaja, his Lordship would exert his good offices with his Highness for the restoration of an amicable un-derstanding between the two Powers. The Maharaja, with the characteristic confidence which he has uniformly placed in the faith and friendship of the British nation, at once assented to the proposition of the Governor-General, to the effect that in the mean time hostilities on his part should be suspended.

"It subsequently came to the knowledge of the Governor-General that a Persian army was besieging Herat; that intrigues were actively prosecuted throughout Afghanistan, for the pur-pose of extending Persian influence and authority to the banks of, and even beyond, the Indus; and that the Court of Persia had not only commenced a course of injury and insult to the of-ficers of Her Majesty's mission in the Persian territory, but had afforded evidence of being engaged in designs wholly at vari-ance with the principles and objects of its alliance with Great Britain.

"After much time spent by Captain Burnes in fruitless nego-tiation at Kabul, it appeared that Dost Mahomed Khan, chiefly in consequence of his reliance upon Persian encouragement and assistance, persisted, as respected his misunderstanding with the Sikhs, in urging the most unreasonable pretensions, such as the Governor-General could not, consistently with. justice and his regard for the friendship of Maharajah Runjeet Singh, be the channel of submitting to the consideration of his Highness; that he avowed schemes of aggrandizement and ambition injurious to the security and peace of the frontiers of India; and that he openly threatened, in furtherance of these schemes, to call in every foreign aid which he could command. Ultimately, he gave his undisguised support to the Persian designs in Afghanistan, of the unfriendly and injurious character of which, as concerned the British power in India, he was well apprised; and by his utter disregard of the views and interests of the British Government compelled Captain Burnes to leave Kabul without having effected any of the objects of his mission.

"It was now evident that no further interference could be exercised by the British Government to bring about a good understanding between the Sikh ruler and Dost Mahomed Khan; and the hostile policy of the latter chief showed too plainly that so long as Kabul remained under his government we could never hope that the tranquillity of our neighbourhood would be secured, or that the interests of our Indian empire would be preserved inviolate.

"The Governor-General deems it in this place necessary to revert to the siege of Herat and the conduct of the Persian nation. The siege of that city had now been carried on by the Persian army for many months. The attack upon it was a most unjustifiable and cruel aggression, perpetrated and continued notwithstanding the solemn and repeated remonstrances of the British envoy at the Court of Persia, and after every just and becoming offer of accommodation had been made and rejected. The besieged have behaved with gallantry and fortitude worthy of the justice of their cause, and the Governor-General would yet indulge the hope that their heroism may enable them to maintain a successful defence until succours shall reach them from British India. In the mean time the ulterior designs of Persia, affecting the interests of the British Government, have been by a succession of events, more and more openly manifested.

"The Governor-General has recently ascertained, by an official despatch from Mr. McNeil, Her Majesty's envoy, that his Excellency has been compelled, by the refusal of his just demands, and by a systematic course of disrespect adopted towards him by the Persian Government, to quit the court of the *shah*, and to make a public declaration of the cessation of all intercourse between the two Governments. The necessity under which Great

Britain is placed of regarding the present advance of the Persian arms into Afghanistan as an act of hostility towards herself, has also been officially communicated to the *shah*, under the express order of Her Majesty's Government.

"The chiefs of Kandahar (brothers of Dost Mahomed Khan, of Kabul) have avowed their adherence to the Persian policy, with the same full knowledge of its opposition to the rights and interests of the British nation in India, and to have been openly assisting in the operations against Herat.

"In the crisis of affairs consequent upon the retirement of our envoy from Kabul, the Governor-General felt the importance of taking immediate measures for arresting the rapid progress of foreign intrigue and aggression towards our own territories.

"His attention was naturally drawn, at this conjuncture, to the position and claims of Shah Soojah-ool-Moolk, a monarch who, when in power, had cordially acceded to the measures of united resistance to external enmity which were, at that time judged necessary by the British Government, and who, on his empire being usurped by its present rulers, had found an honourable asylum in the British dominions.

"It had clearly been ascertained, from the information furnished by the various officers who have, visited Afghanistan, that the Barukzye chiefs, from their disunion and unpopularity, were ill-fitted, under any circumstances, to be useful allies to the British Government, and to aid us in our just and necessary measures of national defence. Yet so long as they refrained from proceedings injurious to our interests and security, the British Government acknowledged and respected their authority. But a different policy appeared to be now more than justified by the conduct of those chiefs, and to be indispensable to our own safety. The welfare of our possessions in the East requires that we should have on our western frontier an ally who is interested in resisting aggression and establishing tranquillity, in the place of chiefs ranging themselves in subservience to a hostile Power, and seeking to promote schemes of conquest and aggrandisement.

"After a serious and mature deliberation, the Governor-Gen-

108

eral was satisfied that pressing necessity, as well as every consideration of policy and justice, warranted us in espousing the cause of Shah Soojah-ool-Moolk, whose popularity throughout Afghanistan had been proved to his Lordship by the strong and unanimous testimony of the best authorities. Having arrived at this determination, The Governor-General was further of opinion that it was just and proper, no less from the position of Maharaja Runjeet Singh, than from his undeviating friendship towards the British Government, that his Highness should have the offer of becoming a party to the contemplated operations. Mr. MacNaghten was accordingly deputed in June last to the Court of his Highness, and the result of his mission has been the conclusion of a tripartite treaty by the British Government, the Maharaja, and Shah Soojah-ool-Moolk, whereby his Highness is guaranteed in his present possessions, and has bound himself to co-operate for the restoration of the *shah* to the throne of his ancestors.

"The friends and enemies of any one of the contracting parties have been declared to be the friends and enemies of all. Various points have been adjusted which had been the subject of discussion between the British Government and his Highness the Maharaja, the identity of whose interests with those of the Honourable Company has now been made apparent to all the surrounding States. A guaranteed independence will, upon favourable conditions, be tendered to the *Ameers* of Scinde; and the integrity of Herat, in the possession of its present ruler, will be fully respected; whilst, by the measures completed or in progress it may reasonably be hoped that the general freedom and security of commerce will be promoted; that the name and just influence of the British Government will gain their proper footing among the nations of central Asia; that tranquillity will be established upon the most important frontier in India, and that a lasting barrier will be raised against hostile intrigue and encroachment.

"His Majesty Shah Soojah-ool-Moolk will enter Afghanistan surrounded by his own troops, and will be supported against foreign interference and factious opposition by a British army. The Governor-General confidently hopes that the Shah will be speedily replaced on his throne by his own subjects and adherents; and when once he shall be secured in power, and the independence and integrity of Afghanistan established, the British army will be withdrawn.

"The Governor-General has been led to these measures by the duty which is imposed upon him of providing for the security of the British Crown; but he rejoices that in the discharge of his duty he will be enabled to assist in restoring the union and prosperity of the Afghan people. Throughout the approaching operations British influence will be sedulously employed to further every measure of general benefit, to reconcile differences, to secure oblivion of injuries, and to put an end to the distractions by which, for so many years, the welfare and happiness of the Afghans have been impaired.

"Even to the chiefs whose hostile proceedings have given just cause of offence to the British Government, it will seek to secure liberal and honourable treatment, on their tendering early submission, and ceasing from opposition to that course of measures which may be judged the most suitable for the general advantage of their country.

"By order of the Right Hon. the Governor-General of India,

"W. H. MacNaghten,

"Secretary to the Government of India,

"With the Governor-General.

"NOTIFICATION

"With reference to the preceding declaration, the following appointments are made;—

"Mr. W. H. MacNaghten, secretary to Government, will assume the functions of envoy and minister, on the part of the Government of India, at the Court of Shah Soojah-ool-Moolk; Mr. MacNaghten will be assisted by the following officers:—

"Captain Alexander Burnes, of the Bombay establishment,

who will be employed under Mr. MacNaghten's direction, as envoy to the chief of Khelat, or other states.

"Lieutenant E. D'Arcy Todd, of the Bengal artillery, to be political assistant and military secretary to the envoy and minister.

"Lieutenant Eldred Pottinger, of the Bombay artillery; Lieutenant R. Leech, of the Bombay Engineers; Mr. P. B. Lord, of the Bombay Medical Establishment, to be political assistants to ditto ditto.

"Lieutenant E. R. Conolly, of the 6th Regiment Bengal Cavalry, to command the escort of the Envoy and Minister, and to be military assistant to ditto ditto.

"Mr. G. J. Berwick, of the Bengal Medical Establishment, to be surgeon to ditto ditto.

"W. H. MacNaghten,

"Secretary to the Governor of India, with the Governor-General."

An Overview of the
Afghan Campaign

In 1838 the British Government of India, which had hitherto never resorted to arms, except in self-defence or upon extreme provocation, suddenly took upon themselves, in defiance of the dictates of reason and justice, to commit an unprovoked assault on a harmless neighbour. This course of action must be attributed primarily to a motive which had as early as the first decade of the nineteenth century begun to exercise the minds of our Indian statesmen and soldiers, and has since that date been ever present with them—the fear of an invasion of India by Russia across the north-west frontier. This fear had at this time become acute, chiefly by reason of a Persian attack, believed to be instigated by Russia, against the Afghan city of Herat, and reported intrigues by Russian emissaries at Cabul. The internal state of Afghanistan itself, which for years had been in a chronic state of internecine strife over the succession to the throne, also seemed to call for some British action to erect a firm barrier to any further Russian enterprise in the direction of India. The immediate danger was in fact absurdly exaggerated, and diplomacy might safely have been left to deal with it. No serious attempt, however, appears to have been made in this direction, and the alarmist views of irresponsible and ignorant men led the Governor-General, Lord Auckland, to adopt another course of action, the wrong-headedness of which was only equalled by its unrighteousness. The existing Amir at Cabul, Dost Mahomed, having declined to accede to our first tentative overtures for alliance, it was decided to supplant him by another claimant to the throne, one Shah Sooja, who had previously held and lost it, and had since proved in several unsuccessful attempts his inability to regain it without outside assistance. He was therefore a convenient tool in our hands ; the Sikhs of the Punjab, inveterate foes of the Afghans, were persuaded to join us in the iniquitous attempt to force a discredited prince on a reluctant people; and the original design, which had at first involved merely the assistance of Shah Sooja with money, arms and officers to train his levies, had swollen by the autumn of 1838 to a large-scale invasion of Afghanistan by British and Sikh forces, on grounds which, even as stated by the aggressors, could only be regarded as of the flimsiest order.

The plan of campaign, as finally drawn up, involved the advance of a large British force, drawn from the Bengal and Bombay armies, and concentrated on the lower Indus, in the nominally friendly territory of the Ameers of Sind, *via* the Bolan Pass and Quetta, on Candahar and Cabul, while a Sikh contingent was to force the Khyber Pass and cooperate against the Afghan capital. Shah Sooja's corps was to move with the British, who, as soon as they had set him upon the throne and effected the relief of Herat, were to evacuate the country and leave him to fend for himself. While the concentration of the "Army of the Indus" was still in process of completion, however, news arrived that the Persians had raised the siege of Herat and were retiring to their own country, thus removing every shred of real justification from the expedition. The governor-general, however, felt that matters had gone too far to allow of its abandonment, and confined himself to reducing by about one-third the force originally destined to take part in it. By the end of 1838 the Bengal contingent, numbering, with Shah Sooja's motley army, 15,000 men, were assembled around Shikarpore, on the west bank of the Indus, while the Bombay troops, 5,000 strong, had effected their landing at the mouth of that river; but further delays were still to occur before the campaign could be opened, owing to the hostility of the Ameers of Sind, who objected— with good reason—to our troops battening on their country, as being contrary to a treaty concluded with them some years before, and by obstructive tactics and even by open opposition strove to throw every possible obstacle in our way. They were eventually overawed by a display of force, and by February 1839, although the Bombay troops had not yet effected their junction with their comrades, Sir John Keane decided to commence his advance with the force at Shikarpore only.

His difficulties sprang not so much from hostile resistance, for as far as Candahar none, and beyond that little more, was met with, as from the inadequate provision of transport and of

115

the supply service for his army, which it must be remembered included two followers and three camels for every fighting man in its ranks. Consequently he only reached Candahar at the end of May, and was compelled there to make a long halt of two months to complete the concentration of his army and replenish his magazines. The march was then resumed; the fortress of Ghazni was surprised and captured despite the absence of the siege train, which had been unwisely left behind at Candahar; and the levies collected by Dost Mahomed for a last gambler's throw lost heart and melted away before the inexorable progress of the invaders. The unhappy Amir fled for refuge to the Hindu Kush mountains, and early in August Shah Sooja was enthroned in his stead on the British entry into Cabul. The bulk of the Afghan forces had in fact been detained far from the decisive point by the menace of a Sikh invasion by way of the Khyber Pass, and dissolved into fragments at the news of the loss of their capital.

Thus an almost bloodless triumph had been won and a large part of Keane's army was forthwith despatched home, Elphinstone with 5,000 men being left in garrison at Cabul, Nott with a similar number at Candahar, and smaller detachments at various places in the centre and east of Afghanistan. But the disturbed state of the country gave ominous proof that our task was as yet but half fulfilled, and that Shah Sooja's power, resting as it did only on British bayonets, must collapse if deprived of that support. The dethroned Amir collected his forces in the heart of his mountain fortress, and made more than one bold attempt to retrieve his lost fortunes; the tribes between Cabul and Candahar rose en masse, and an insurrection of the Baluchis menaced our communications by way of Quetta with the Indus. Full employment was afforded the British flying columns throughout the spring and summer of 1840 in dealing with those various centres of unrest, but in November the surrender of Dost Mahomed, at the very moment when his affairs were apparently taking a turn for the better, seemed to presage a speedy end to our troubles. Although many of the tribes still remained in the field during the early part of 1841, by the autumn the state of the country seemed to be approximating to its normal degree of quietude—never very great,—the relief of part of the army of occupation was ordered, administrative economies were enforced, and the British subsidies to the tribal chiefs were drastically cut down. Dread of Russian designs in Central Asia was, however, still lively, and this, and the realisation in Government circles that Shah Sooja was still too weak to stand alone, combined to forbid for the present the complete withdrawal of the British army from Afghan territory. But a fearful Nemesis was now hard at hand.

In October, with a suddenness and simultaneity which pointed clearly to pre-arrangement, the whole of the occupied area flamed up in rebellion. Sale's brigade, marching back from Cabul to India on relief, was vigorously assailed in the passes, and compelled to throw itself for safety into Jellalabad. Nott in Candahar was closely beset by hordes of tribesmen and had to fight hard and frequently to rid himself of them; an attempt to bring supplies to him from Quetta was beaten back, and the garrison of Ghazni was rapidly and effectively invested and driven into the citadel of the place. It was at Cabul, however, that the hapless tools of an iniquitous policy requited to the full the sins of their rulers. Elphinstone, who was physically and temperamentally unequal to the demands of his difficult position, did nothing effective to deal with the rising in the city. He let himself be deprived of his stores and shut up in indefensible cantonments, and refused to sally forth from them either to revenge the murder of his political officers, or to redeem his own army from destruction by the only honourable and possible means. Akbar, the favourite son of Dost Mahomed, had now assumed chief control of the insurgents, and with him there was at length concluded a disgraceful treaty, by which the British signed away everything they still held and agreed to withdraw from the country at the bare price of their lives. The terms were not and perhaps were never meant to be observed, and barely a week after Elphinstone's demoralised and half-starved regiments had set out on their *via* Dolorosa, a solitary survivor arrived at Jellalabad to tell

117

of the utter destruction of the whole British army.

So staggered were the Government by this unexpected catastrophe, which shed a lurid and baleful light over the last days of Auckland's term of office, that for a while no serious attempt was made to retrieve them. The fate of the Ghazni garrison, who in March 1842 surrendered on terms and were at once massacred, was all but shared by that of Jellalabad, the commander of which, a premature attempt at his relief having miscarried, was only withheld from asking for terms by the vigorous opposition of the junior member of his council of war, Broadfoot. And in fact the new Governor-General, Lord Ellenborough, had at first no design beyond the safe withdrawal of the "illustrious garrison" and the force at Candahar, leaving British men and women prisoners in Afghan hands and British honour trailed in the dust. Fortunately George Pollock, the cool-headed and resolute commander of the relieving army now collecting at Peshawar, had other and less timid views. Owing to the low morale of many of his regiments, and the difficulty of collecting sufficient supplies, it was April before he could force his way through the Khyber Pass and effect his junction with Sale at Jellalabad. Akbar's investment of the latter place had been neither incessant nor vigorous, the greatest danger to the garrison having been from an earthquake which overthrew all their defences, and a few days before Pollock's arrival the Afghan besieging army had been totally defeated by a sortie. A long pause of four months now ensued, while the Governor-General was debating in his own mind and discussing with his generals the alternative policies of advance to Cabul to restore British prestige, and evacuation of the country. In the end he left the choice to Pollock and Nott as to whether they would retire "by way of Cabul", which they eagerly decided to do. Accordingly this strange "retreat" was commenced both from Jellalabad and Candahar in August. The hostile forces who endeavoured to oppose Pollock were handsomely beaten at Tezin, and Nott in his turn defeated his immediate adversaries south-west of Ghazni. On September 15 Pollock, anticipating his colleague by a few hours, took possession of the capital city, which thus fell for the second time in three years into our hands; and suitable vengeance was taken for our previous humiliations and disasters. Ellenborough was in no way inclined to repeat the errors of his predecessor by sanctioning any prolonged stay in Afghanistan, and by the end of 1842 the victorious armies were back once more in British territory. The hapless Shah Sooja having been assassinated some time before, there seemed no better solution to the question of the succession to the throne than the restoration of the deposed Dost Mahomed. To him was therefore generously given back what we should never have taken from him.

The disasters of the first Afghan War dealt to our arms a blow the echo of which resounded throughout India and the East; but that they were at all possible must be attributed rather to the faults of the political authorities and the higher command than to any decline in the fighting value of the troops, who nobly redeemed their tarnished reputation under Pollock, Nott and Sale. The political objects of the war, however, remained even in the end unachieved, and indeed its result was on the whole rather disadvantageous to us than otherwise. The Russian menace, such as it was, remained as potent a bogey as ever; the ruler and people of Afghanistan were left willing to wound if afraid to strike; and our enemies in the East suddenly realised with wonder and hope that the hitherto irresistible might of Britain had, like Achilles, a vulnerable heel.

9 781846 775673